Lessons Learned from an Unconventional Design for Lean Six Sigma Deployment

What Worked, What Didn't and How We Were Able to Create, Develop and Implement Design for Lean Six Sigma into Xerox Corporation's Product Design Community

Norman E. Fowler

Lessons Learned from an Unconventional Design for Lean Six Sigma Deployment

Published by Lulu Press, Incorporated
860 Aviation Parkway, Suite 300
Morrisville, NC 27560

ISBN 978-1-4357-0824-2

Author and Editor: Norman E. Fowler

Author and copyright owner can be contacted at:
Keys Six Sigma, Incorporated
824 Terry Lane
Key West, FL 33040
normfowler@keys6sigma.com

Contents

Forward

When I first met Norm Fowler, he had recently been assigned the responsibility of leading the Design for Lean Six Sigma (DfLSS) rollout at Xerox. This new assignment created numerous and extensive challenges. Like many organizations, Xerox had developed multiple opinions with regard to strategy and approach. Norm had the additional challenge of multiple design organizations with different leaders across geographically diverse locations, ranging from coast to coast and encompassing various locations in Europe and South America. The goal was lofty: roll out DfLSS to all of Xerox's 4,500 engineers across the disciplines of electro-mechanical, chemical, software, physics, and more.

While Norm's challenges were exceptional, his performance easily surmounted them. Perhaps his greatest achievement was working effectively with the various groups within Xerox, bringing concurrence on approach and strategy. He also directed resources to specific design organizations that would embrace DfLSS, thereby providing examples of success to motivate the less enthusiastic. Norm worked with the consultants and trainers in customizing the materials and methods to better integrate DfLSS tools and techniques into Xerox's culture and existing engineering expertise. Finally, his certification strategy served as a bridge between training and everyday practice. As a result of Norm's leadership, the DfLSS deployment at Xerox is one of the most pervasive, broadly applied, and successful programs in US history.

To our benefit, Norm has written this book to share his expertise and experiences at Xerox during the DfLSS rollout. This book contains rich and detailed information on how to effectively lead a DfLSS deployment. He has shared multiple strategies on building concurrence, managing service providers, structuring certification, and dealing with multiple engineering disciplines. While many books are written in a style full of buzzword-babble that communicates no concepts nor provides any insight – and yet consumes hundreds of pages – Norm engages this topic in a clear, well-written style that is both easy to read and exceptionally helpful. If you are involved in, or contemplating a DfLSS deployment, this book is a must-read. *Lessons Learned from an Unconventional Design for Lean Six Sigma Deployment* provides a blueprint for success.

Philip Mayfield

Preface

When I left Xerox in 2007, we were in the third year of Xerox Corporation's Design for Lean Six Sigma (or DfLSS) deployment. From all internal accounts and from the few external to Xerox who were familiar with our deployment, we exceeded most, if not all, of the expectations we had when we started. Through dedicated hard work by a whole host of very talented people, we were able to take a different perspective on how to set up and deploy a DfLSS program to a product design community that were somewhat hesitant to fully embrace the DMAIC (Define, Measure, Analyze, Improve and Control) Lean Six Sigma initiative. As I was leaving, I thought it would be a shame not to capture what worked, what did not and what lessons the design and deployment community learned through the process. This book is an attempt to capture that critical learning in hopes that internally we retain what was learned and those external may gain some valuable insight from Xerox's experiences.

In mid 2003, I joined the Xerox Corporate Lean Six Sigma Office staff as the senior staff process owner of the DMAIC Green Belt program. Earlier that year, Xerox had kicked off their Lean Six Sigma program with their first few waves of Black Belt training. Though we were following a fairly scripted deployment recipe, it was clear that we were going to take advantage of new thinking and ideas to enhance the Xerox deployment. The DMAIC Green Belt was a good example. We realized that if we were going to make significant inroads in enhancing the Xerox culture, DMAIC Green Belts were going to be essential in the long run. The one percent of the Xerox population that were going to be Black Belts would have an impact initially by delivering projects and results and in the longer term as they rotated back into the operations. However, they would still be a small minority of the overall Xerox population. If we were going to have a major impact on the culture, it would be by training and mobilizing a significant portion of the population as Green Belts.

Rolling out the DMAIC Green Belt program faced several geographic and other obstacles. So, we decided early to use a blended training approach where a majority of the Six Sigma tools and DMAIC process was taught via a self paced, on-line program and the Lean methods were taught in a more classic classroom training environment. The blended training model was somewhat new for Xerox as well as our consulting partners, but we made it work. It was that willingness to try new things, not accept the "cookie cutter" approaches other companies used and focus on the Voice of the Customer that enabled a fresh look a developing and deploying the Xerox Design for Lean Six Sigma program.

Design for Lean Six Sigma Troika

Though the DMAIC Green Belt program was important to Xerox, I joined the Corporate Lean Six Sigma Senior Staff to play a significant role in developing and deploying the Design for Lean Six Sigma program within the product development and delivery organizations. Given Xerox's decentralized research, design and engineering structure, it was difficult to drive an initiative like DfLSS without help. This was not an exception. Two of my key partners, Heidi Grenek and Eduardo Bascaran, worked in the Xerox Engineering Center, a centralized staff function aimed at enhancing the engineering and product delivery capability. For purposes of this book, I'll refer to the three of us as the "DfLSS Troika." The term troika is a Russian word defined in Merriam-Webster's online dictionary as "a Russian vehicle drawn by three horses abreast; *also*: a team for such a vehicle. A group of three; *especially*: an administrative or ruling body of three." [i] The definition fits as the three of us grabbed the DfLSS program reins and rode it through the first three years of its deployment.

To make this work the way it did, it took the efforts of many other people from all different organizations. It was truly a collaborative process that brought out the innovation, creativity and teamwork of Xerox employees. Another key player was Pat Waara, who played a major role in the development and delivery of the Software DfLSS initiative and as a practical voice of reason on the entire DfLSS initiative. Together, with the support and help from countless others, we established a framework for deploying DfLSS across an entire organization focused not only on technical and process issues, but also those associated with the program's sustainability and pervasiveness.

Why This Deployment is Considered "Unconventional?"

I call this deployment "unconventional" because it did not follow other noted deployment recipes. Xerox's Lean Six Sigma deployment could be viewed as a standard recipe: a prescribed number of Black Belts and a greater number of Green Belts, management training, dedicated infrastructure to support the deployment, etc. From most accounts, this recipe served Xerox well as we embarked on our Lean Six Sigma journey. However, as the DfLSS "troika" examined our customers, the product delivery teams, and their needs we saw some shortfalls in the standard Lean Six Sigma deployment strategies. Our intent was to build on the positive aspects we saw and look for new ways to overcome the shortfalls as we deployed to this unique group of people.

Seeing is Believing

In my career spanning almost 27 years at Xerox, I held a number of positions with Xerox ranging from manufacturing technology, business strategy to running a large "full service supplier" operation which included research, design and multinational manufacturing under one organization. The combination of these positions helped me prepare for my last position within the Lean Six Sigma organization as they provided a broad exposure to Xerox product development and delivery as well as the population we ultimately would be serving with Design for Lean Six Sigma. It was back in my days leading the manufacturing technology organization in the mid to late 1990's that I experienced first hand the power of the DfLSS tool set and methodology. Our organization was chartered to develop and deliver the manufacturing technologies for critical components for Xerox's iGen3® machine. These components had sub-micron tolerances and characteristics which made them *almost* un-manufacturable. Through a series of Design of Experiments (DoE's), Measurement System Analysis (MSA) and use of other DfLSS methods and tools, we were able to not only identify the critical process drivers, but design, build and operate state of the art manufacturing facilities to meet these tough tolerances. From this experience, I learned the power of these techniques and how they enable product delivery organizations to delivery customer-centric designs effectively, effectively and predictably. When the Lean Six Sigma Office was established, I was asked to come on board to support a company-wide Design for Lean Six Sigma deployment across all product delivery related disciplines. This book highlights our journey down this unconventional path. It includes what we found worked, what did not and how we were able to get Design for Lean Six Sigma embedded into a significant portion of Xerox's research, design and development organizations.

The Book Structure

I have divided this book into four chapters. The first three chapters are generally in chronological order. The intent here was to capture the series of events and the decisions made along the way. Chapter One describes Xerox's Quality legacy and how that critical foundation led to and supported the deployment of the Lean Six Sigma initiative. Chapter Two focuses on how the stage was set

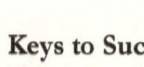

Keys to Success

Through out the book there will be this graphic which will have some tips and additional insights that may help you in your deployments.

for the Design for Lean Six Sigma initiative. Chapter Three goes into detail on how Xerox developed and ultimately deployed Design for Lean Six Sigma to the product delivery community. Chapter Four outlines a series of lessons learned from our Design for Lean Six Sigma experiences. Along the way, there will be a several "Keys to Success" graphics that are short tips, comments, and suggestions that may assist that may assist you as you are contemplating, developing or deploying your own Design for Lean Six Sigma initiative. I hope you enjoy the book.

---

[i] Merriam-Webster Online Dictionary, http://www.merriam-webster.com/

About the Author

Norman Fowler is the President of Keys Six Sigma, Incorporated (www.keys6sigma.com). Keys Six Sigma, Inc. is a consulting firm focused on working with clients to develop and deploy customized Lean Six Sigma and Design for Lean Six Sigma programs that meet their unique needs.

Prior to starting Keys Six Sigma, Mr. Fowler worked 27 years at Xerox Corporation where he held several technology development, strategic planning and managerial assignments. In mid-2003, Norm joined the Xerox's Corporate Lean Six Sigma staff as Manager of Strategic Initiatives. His initial responsibilities include development and deployment of the DMAIC Green Belt and Design for Lean Six Sigma-Process (DMEDI) programs. For the last several years, Norman has been responsible for developing and deploying the Design for Lean Six Sigma-Product (IDOV) initiative. Prior to his Lean Six Sigma assignment, Mr. Fowler was the Manager of Fuser Delivery Unit. The Fuser Delivery Unit is a Xerox multinational Full Service Supplier that designs, develops and manufactures fuser modules and components as well as other critical xerographic components.

Mr. Fowler holds an Associates degree in Plastics Technology from the State University of New York at Morrisville. He graduated Summa Cum Laude with a Bachelor of Science degree in Plastics Engineering and holds a Masters of Science degree in Plastics from the University of Lowell, Lowell, Massachusetts.

Acknowledgements

This book is a result of the innovation, hard work and dedication of a great number of my colleagues and other outside partners who developed and implemented the Xerox Design for Lean Six Sigma initiative. Without their efforts the overall program and this book would not have been possible. I greatly appreciate all of the inputs, coaching and counseling they provided along the way.

It is impossible to list everyone who contributed to making this Design for Lean Six Sigma initiative successful. However, there are a few individuals that I would like to single out for their contributions to the overall Design for Lean Six Sigma program and me personally:

- Heidi Grenek and Eduardo Bascaran - My Design for Lean Six Sigma Troika partners whose unique insight, dedication and hard work made this program reality. You both made the Design for Lean Six Sigma development and deployment exciting, challenging and great fun!

- Pat Waara - Thank you for counsel, insight and the patience you showed while convincing me and others that Software Design for Lean Six Sigma was "different."

- Art Fornari - Thank you for your Lean Six Sigma leadership and giving me the chance to take the Design for Lean Six Sigma methods and principles to the broader Xerox design and development community.

- Nancy Rees - Thank you for your Lean Six Sigma leadership and support when I was faced tough career decisions.

- Sophie Vandebroek – Thank you for your leadership, enthusiasm and dedication advocating for the Xerox engineering community.

- George Maszle - Thank you for your insight, willingness to listen to my brainstorm ideas and being a role model Quality professional.

- Debbie Stocker, Judy Beach and Mary Ellen Campbell - Thank you for all your support. Too often Administrative Assistants do not get the credit they deserve.

- Greg Kovacs, Lou Schneider, Jamie Soley and Tom Wesner - These are the initial Design for Lean Six Sigma Deployment Managers who helped provide critical inputs from the design and development community rank and file and helped drive Design for Lean Six Sigma into their respective organizations.

- Jean Tajc - Thank you for your insight, technical depth and "can-do" attitude.

- Sharon Mathiason - Thank you for your ground-breaking Master Black Belt projects, support for the Software Design for Lean Six Sigma initiative and your discipline approach in all you do.

- Jane Kanehl and Bruce Parks - Thank you for your Xerox contributions, inspiration and friendship for the last 25 years.

- Al Monahan - Thank you for your leadership, vision and role model behavior early on in my Xerox career. You showed me that task and people management can coexist and you should strive for quality and discipline in everything you do.

- Mark Kiemele from Air Academy Associates - Thank you for your infectious Lean Six Sigma passion and keen insight as it made an impact on Xerox's management team.

- Philip Mayfield from SigmaZone.com and Air Academy Associates - Thank you for your technical depth, innovative thinking and willingness to try new things.

- Xerox Advance Engineering and Manufacturing Center and Fuser Delivery Unit personnel - A special thank you to everyone who worked with me to demonstrate that the Design for Lean Six Sigma methods and tools work. You all proved that if you take outstanding people armed with Design for Lean Six Sigma tools and discipline, you can achieve the impossible.

Saving the most important for last, I want to thank my wife Sue for all her support over the last twenty-six years. I am confident that without her dedication, devotion and love I would not be where I am today.

Chapter 1

A Quality Legacy Builds a Solid Foundation

How Leadership Through Quality and other Quality initiatives built a strong foundation for Design for Lean Six Sigma

Starting with Leadership Through Quality- Xerox's Quality Journey Without a Finish Line.

Xerox Corporation has a long and storied Quality-oriented past which served as a solid foundation and an evolutionary springboard for the Xerox Lean Six Sigma and Design for Lean Six Sigma initiatives. Back in the 1970's Xerox implemented quality circles and various employee involvement initiatives. It was not until the early 1980's, when faced with stiff competition from Japanese and other business equipment manufacturers, then Chief Executive Officer (CEO) David Kearns and the senior management team adopted a corporate-wide Total Quality Management initiative known as "Leadership Through Quality." Leadership Though Quality was a corporate wide, customer-centric program that included such topics as understanding customer requirements, a six step Problem Solving Process, a multi-step Quality Improvement Process, an introduction to effective team interactive stills and competitive benchmarking. Over a three year period, over 100,000 employees received the 28 hours of training which took more than four million people-hours and $125 million to deliver.[i]

The Xerox Problem Solving Process, or PSP as it was known, involved the following phase-gated six steps: (1) identifying a problem, (2) analyzing that problem, (3) generating potential solutions, (4) selecting

1

and planning that solution, (5) implementing the solution and (6) evaluating the solution. One may argue that this basic problem solving framework is very similar to today's Lean Six Sigma DMAIC process. The Quality Improvement Process (or QIP) consisted of three main sections: Planning, Organizing and Monitoring for Quality. Planning for Quality included identifying the output and customers, getting the customer requirements and translating those requirements to specifications. Organizing for Quality included identifying the steps in the process, selecting measurements and determining process capability. If the customer specification could be met with the existing process, one would go directly to monitoring. If not, one would exit and utilize the above mentioned Problem Solving Process to attack the gap to the customers' specification. In Monitoring the Process, one would evaluate the results and assess if there were any problems. If there were, again one would exit to the Problem Solving Process to resolve the issues. If not, one would exit and recycle back to Planning for Quality with an understanding of process capability and any gaps that need to be closed.

Keys to Success

Having a committed senior leadership always helps in any change initiative deployment. Without it, the deployment task gets much more difficult!

The Quality Improvement Process focused on process discipline, translation of the customer requirements to supplier specifications and reinforced that customer satisfaction was the responsibility of every employee. Like in many of today's Lean Six Sigma deployments, employees were required to demonstrate their mastery of the overall tools and processes by completing a management approved project. Along with the "hard", process driven skills there were also training sections on interactive skills and teamwork. These included basic techniques for effectively interacting in a team environment such as initiating, clarifying and reacting to people on teams in a constructive manner. Also included was content on empowerment, giving each Xerox employee the responsibility to identify and correct problems that impacted quality in our products and services.

One novel aspect of Leadership Through Quality was its "top-down" deployment led by the David Kearns and the corporation's senior management. After the CEO and the senior management were trained, they in turn played a key role and participated in the training of their respective staffs. This waterfall training model continued down the corporate ladder until each organization worldwide was trained. This waterfall technique proved to be very powerful, ensuring pervasiveness across and within organizations and encouraged sustainability of the process use over time.

Through the next several years teams were established, Quality Improvement Projects were conducted and millions of dollars of savings were realized. Just as important as the savings, Leadership Through Quality became the way we worked. Everyone understood the terms, processes and tools and used them on a daily basis. It became how we talked and interacted with one another. Every employee began to focus on their customers and how their actions impacted the overall customer experience.

As a result of the Leadership Through Quality initiative, overall customer satisfaction jumped 40 percent and customer complaints decreased 60 percent. By the late 1980's, 75 percent of Xerox workers participated in the quest to improve quality and 7,000 quality improvement teams were formed.[ii] The foundation of Leadership Through Quality formed the basis for Xerox winning the National Institute of Standards and Technology's Malcolm Baldrige National Quality Award in 1989. Over the next several years, Xerox won a significant number of international

Quality awards, including a second Malcolm Baldrige Award for the Xerox Business Services in 1997.

In the mid 1990's another Xerox initiative became a building block for Design for Lean Six Sigma (DfLSS). Launched by then Xerox's Chief Engineer Maurice Holmes, Xerox's Engineering Excellence Institute began to train engineers in Quality Functional Deployment (QFD), Taguchi Robust Design and many other tools and techniques currently associated with many DfLSS programs. Theses skills were intended to support Xerox's Time To Market process. The Time To Market process is a structured, phase-gate business process intended to guide consistent and disciplined product delivery. As with many product development processes, Xerox's Time To Market broke the development initiative into several phases, each with a set of exit criteria and recommended evidence for passing each gate. The Time To Market process also provided management with a framework for assessing program risks, progress at mitigating those risks and overall program direction.

In the mid to late 1990's, other Quality initiatives were initiated within Xerox's manufacturing and supply chain communities. In 1998, Xerox initiated Operational Quality. Driven by Al Monahan, Vice President of Manufacturing Support, Operational Quality could be considered Xerox's first step into formal Lean and Six Sigma training. Like many such initiatives in other companies, Operational Quality began in the manufacturing operations where data were easily obtainable, personnel were familiar with the tools and techniques and there was senior management support for ongoing productivity and process improvement. Initially, several "waves" of skilled candidates were identified and trained over several weeks in classical Lean and Six Sigma techniques. There were also one-week training classes for management. Over time, other elements such as on-line tool training were added to give a broader exposure to Operational Quality within and outside of the manufacturing and supply chain organizations. As awareness of its effectiveness spread, Al Monahan offered up these highly trained engineers to work outside his organization to tackle critical nontechnical business problems facing Xerox at the time.

Deploying Xerox's Lean Six Sigma Initiative

As Xerox entered into the new millennium, it was mired in a failed attempt to reorganize Xerox's sales force, a prolonged Securities and Exchange Commission (SEC) investigation of questionable accounting practices and in a failing, costly business model that then President Anne Mulcahy declared "unsustainable." On the brink of declaring bankruptcy, in August, 2001 Xerox named Anne Mulcahy as Chief Executive Officer. By late, 2002 the SEC accounting issues were resolved and dramatic efforts had been taken to reduce operating expenditures, improve operational efficiency and slash the company's debt. Though Anne and her senior leadership team could see their way back to good, there were still barriers to becoming great again. In late

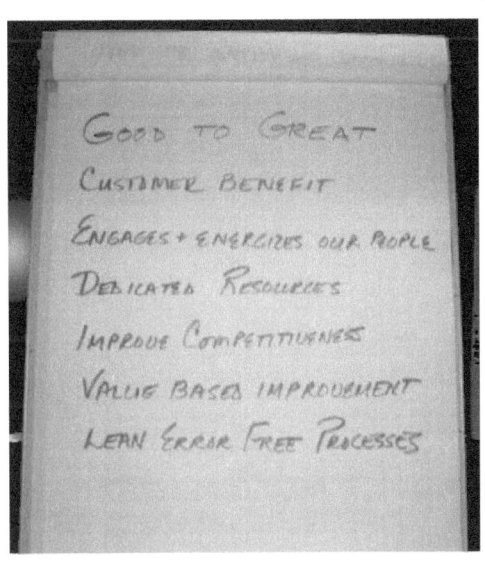

Figure 1.1: Flip Chart Outlining Key Xerox Lean Six Sigma Communication Themes

November, 2002, Anne, her staff and other key Xerox leaders went through Lean Six Sigma (LSS) management training conducted by our DMAIC consulting partner the George Group. At that meeting, they were exposed to Lean Six Sigma techniques and placed in a simulation where they could immediately see and feel the impact of applying these tools and techniques. The Xerox's participants committed the Corporation to Lean Six Sigma by agreeing to a standard "recipe" for deployment, as well as committing the talent and infrastructure resources necessary to be successful. Figure 1.1 outlines the original Xerox Lean Six Sigma communication themes generated by the Xerox Leadership Team during that first workshop.[iii] Anne and her staff also developed three main goals for the Xerox Lean Six Sigma deployment. They were (a) capture the financial benefits associated with Lean Six Sigma projects, (b) enhance the Xerox culture and (c) better prepare the future leaders of the Corporation by training, coaching and returning highly skilled people back into the operations. These three goals are still in place five years later. The DMAIC deployment "recipe" documented in November, 2002 included the following:

- Select projects based on value creation opportunity (Return on Invested Capital (ROIC)/Economic Profit), with number of projects in process controlled.
- Adopt a consistent financial results tracking approach as determined by the deployment team and the financial organization.
- Assign demonstrated top performers to full-time roles.
- Adopt a defined organization structure to enable success.
- Deploy and train resources in roles as defined (full time Black Belts, full time Deployment Managers, Sponsors, Green Belts) using consistent training.
- Engage operations leadership in the process and have them integrate Lean Six Sigma into daily operations.
- Commit at least 0.5 percent of employee population as Black Belts in 2003 and another 0.5 percent in 2004 to achieve critical mass towards our transformation.

This recipe was taken to heart and deployed across the entire Xerox enterprise. Return on Invested Capital (ROIC or Economic Profit) was implemented and used to assess projects, certify Black Belts and track organization performance. ROIC remained a key metric until late, 2006 when it was replaced by Profit Before Tax (PBT). The switch to PBT was driven by confusion outside the Lean Six Sigma community on ROIC and by concern that important projects were being overlooked since they head minimal ROIC benefit. A Project Tracking System (or PTS) was established with the blessing and support of the Finance community. This system tracked each project through the DMAIC or other Lean Six Sigma processes tracking project's financials and activities, as well as serving as a repository of key project information. The information could be rolled up to the top of the Lean Six Sigma

Keys to Success

Integrating Lean *and* Six Sigma up front prevented non-value added debate later on which one of the two were more important. Both are essential for overall productivity and have a synergistic effect when applied together.

operation or to any designated organization. The retrieval system allowed Belts, Deployment Managers and other key people the ability to search, identify and replicate projects which solved similar issues or closed comparable performance gaps.

The appropriate Lean Six Sigma infrastructure was established to enable success. Chief Executive Officer Anne Mulcahy asked Art Fornari to lead the Corporate Lean Six Sigma deployment. A highly tenured Xerox employee, Art had his roots in Xerox's manufacturing, purchasing and distribution organizations. Prior to this assignment, Art was the Senior Vice President of Xerox's North American Manufacturing and Logistics Operations. In his new role, Art reported directly to Anne, sending the message that Lean Six Sigma was an important corporate strategy and initiative.

The intent was to keep the centralized Lean Six Sigma Office staff as *lean* as possible; therefore, starting out there was only a small staff supporting the development and deployment of Lean Six Sigma. The Corporate Lean Six Sigma office included Human Relations (HR) to work with Business Units to select the right Black Belt and Master Black Belt candidates, Finance to manage the Project Tracking System, Logistics to manage the scheduling and execution of training, two senior staff members to manage the overall curriculum and deployment and the manager of the Corporation's Master Black Belts (MBB). The centralized group of Corporate Master Black Belts was established to (a) lead broad, cross-organization projects, (b) serve as the group that would ultimately take over the instruction from our consulting partners and (c) own the certification process. Though this group started out modestly in size, it grew as Xerox took over the training portion of our Xerox deployment, overall training demand increased worldwide and Corporate Master Black Belts began to complete their assignments and roll back into operations. This roll-off impacted the number of Master Black Belts due to the time necessary to bring a Master Black Belt candidate to the point where they could effectively teach and conduct projects.

The Corporate Lean Six Sigma staff basically had two key functions: *support* the deployment of Lean Six Sigma and *govern* the Lean Six Sigma initiative. At times, some believed these two were in conflict, but in reality, they supported one another. The governance role was primarily to help set and uphold policies across the Corporation and its various units. These would include things such as certification requirements and other standards to ensure consistency. The support function was primarily aimed at the unit leaders as well as the Deployment Managers. Each unit of a certain size or function had a full time, dedicated Lean Six Sigma Deployment Manager. These Deployment Managers reported directly to the unit's leader (dotted line to Art Fornari, the Corporate Lean Six Sigma leader), owned the deployment of Lean Six Sigma in their respective organizations and had all of the Black Belts and Master Black Belts reporting to them. Deployment Managers typically were well respected within their organizations and considered high performers. They played a key role in managing the Lean Six Sigma belts, helping the senior leadership teams select the right projects and ensuring that Lean Six Sigma was permeating through their organization. Their ultimate goal was to embed Lean Six Sigma through their entire organization and make it the way their senior team and organization's employees worked. It was the Corporate Lean Six Sigma Office's responsibility to support them in their quest.

The training portion of this recipe varied depending on the depth and breadth of knowledge transferred and the type of training classes selected. Xerox had four levels of DMAIC Lean Six Sigma belts: Yellow Belt, Green Belt, Black Belt and Master Black Belt. Each had a different competency level and training mechanism. The Yellow Belt was not considered a certification level, but a class completion. All the Yellow Belt training was done via an on-line interactive training program developed by MoreSteam.com and tailored to meet Xerox's needs. The training consisted of three sessions with each session having training, interactive exercises and a multiple choice quiz. In order to get credit for the class, students had to cumulatively score 80 percent or better on the quizzes. The training time was estimated at 13 hours, but varied depending on a candidate's skill level, experience and other factors. Class registration was self selecting as any full time Xerox employee could sign up and take the on-line course any time. The basic Yellow Belt program was also translated into six languages to enable easier transfer of knowledge to the majority of Xerox's worldwide employment base.

At the other end of the Xerox Lean Six Sigma training spectrum were the DMAIC Black Belt and Master Black Belt curricula. Unlike the Yellow Belt training, Black Belt candidates needed to go through a robust selection process. Black Belt candidates came from an organization's high performer list. Candidates were typically nominated by management, selected by the organization's top management and validated by the Corporate Lean Six Sigma Office. The intent was to train the best and brightest within Xerox as Black Belts and return them into the operations to help drive Lean Six Sigma through the Corporation. The DMAIC Black Belt training consisted of five weeks of instructor lead training. Knowing that working effectively in teams would be a critical skill, the Black Belt training started with a week of "soft skill" training around how each candidate worked in a team setting. This training was built around Meredith Belbin's work back in the 1970's.[iv] In this first training week, the candidates are introduced to the Belbin philosophy, receive feedback from their work environment on their personal styles and have the opportunity to practice interactive skills in a "safe" environment.

Keys to Success

The "hard" DMAIC and DfLSS statistical skills are often easier to learn, but the "soft" skills (e.g. Team Accelerator) can be more difficult to master.

Approximately a month later, the Black Belt candidates began their four, one week training sessions on Lean and Six Sigma methods and tools. In conjunction with instructor-led training, candidates participated in various simulations, case studies and "teachbacks." The teachbacks proved to be an effective instructional tool. Belt candidates were assigned areas taught during the week and armed with flip charts and markers, they were required to complete a presentation and teach key points of those assigned areas back to the rest of the class prior as preparation for the weekly quiz. The weekly quiz consists of series of multiple choice questions. To successfully pass these quizzes, belt candidates needed to attain at least an 80% correct score. Those who do not meet the 80 percent threshold were provided incremental coaching between training weeks to ensure they have met and mastered the concepts they missed before moving to the next training week. Some may ask why test the belt candidates? From our perspective, testing is a way to assess how much information has been transferred, is another cycle of learning for the candidates and it identifies candidates who may need some remedial help and support between each week of training.

The training sessions were separated by roughly a month, which was intended to be the time between various phases of their first Black Belt DMAIC project which they worked in parallel. The last week of training culminated with a quiz integrating all the weeks of training. With successful completion of the training and quizzes, Black Belts moved on to DMAIC certification. To be a certified, Xerox Black Belts were required to successfully complete the training (with 80 percent or better on the quizzes), complete at least two projects which total $500,000 in Economic Profit (EP) and receive the endorsement from their Master Black Belt coach and Deployment Manager. As in many deployments, the Black Belt level is the most involved and demanding of the three training levels.

The Master Black Belt program was reserved for highly skilled Black Belts who demonstrated leadership and desire to take on an expanded role in the Lean Six Sigma deployment. Most of the Master Black Belt training was focused on preparing candidates to become effective instructors. This included training in fundamental instruction techniques and detailed reviews of the Lean Six Sigma training content. To be a certified Xerox Master Black Belt, candidates needed to teach a one week DMAIC Green Belt class as well as a four week DMAIC Black Belt wave. In addition, candidates needed to complete their DMAIC Black Belt certification, deliver three Master Black Belt-level projects, coach an equivalent of eight Black Belts through their projects and receive the endorsement of their unit's Deployment Manager on their ability to lead and work in a team environment.

The DMAIC Green Belt program had elements of both the Yellow Belt and Black Belt programs. Similar to the Black Belts, the Green Belts were not self selecting as candidates had to be nominated by their management and approved by their Lean Six Sigma Deployment Managers. In general, the number of Green

Keys to Success

Though DMAIC Black Belts are important, in the long haul raising the skills of the general population with Green Belt training and coaching should have a greater overall impact on sustainability and making it the way an organization works.

Belt candidates was somewhat limited early on by the number of Black Belts necessary to coach the Green Belts and the Black Belts' overall process capability to coach. The DMAIC Green Belt training was developed around a blended learning environment. The blended learning environment included both on-line as well as instructor-led portions. The on-line portion of the training included nine sessions primarily focused on Six Sigma tools and methods as well as a module on overall leadership. As in the Yellow Belt sessions, the content was interactive, included links to other web-based information and incorporated a multiple choice quiz at the end of the session.

There were two basic Green Belt on-line curriculums: Service and Technical. As the name would suggest, the Service Green Belt curriculum was aimed for those within Xerox that were conducting service-oriented functions. The Service Green Belt curriculum was quoted at roughly 56 training hours (but for most, it took less time) to complete the nine modules. The Technical Green Belt path was primarily intended for research, development, design and other technology-related Green Belt candidates. This curriculum had eleven sessions and was estimated at 113 hours. In general, the Technical Green Belt content included the Service Green Belt material, but added two modules that significantly expanded the topics of hypothesis testing and Design of Experiments (DoEs). Green Belt candidates had the option to select either on-line curriculum as a prerequisite to the instructor-led training. To no one's surprise, the majority of those who completed Green Belt training took the Service Green Belt content.

Keys to Success
On-line training offers low cost per person, a high degree of message standardization and training flexibility (e.g. time, pace, location, etc.). A blended learning environment (on-line and instructor-led) offers some distinct advantages.

Once a candidate successfully passed the on-line content, they could register for the instructor-led portion of the program. This consisted of one week of training in predominately Lean-related topics like Process Cycle Time, Process mapping, Work In Process (WIP) caps, 5S, etc. and touched upon a few Six Sigma topics such as control charts. In looking back on the decision to approach Green Belt training in this hybrid manner there were several positives. First, the "mechanically-oriented" Six Sigma content could be learned and absorbed at each student's individual pace. For those already knowledgeable in these topics, they could move through the sessions at an accelerated pace. For those who needed more time, they could take it. By the time each of the candidates got to the instructor-led portion of the training; they had all been exposed to a common set of Six Sigma tools that they could build on. Second, we found that for many people the Lean concepts were counterintuitive and difficult to internalize with only on-line instruction. We found that Lean principles were better taught face-to-face in an instructor led environment with breakout exercises where belt candidates could "feel" and "see" the impact of applying Lean to various situations.

Green Belt certification required successful completion of the training (both on-line and instructor-led), completion of a DMAIC project and recommendation by their Black Belt coach. In their DMAIC project, Green Belt candidates needed to demonstrate competency in five Lean Six Sigma tools, with two of those tools being a SIPOC (Supplier, Input, Process, Output, and Customer) and process mapping.

By early 2005 Xerox had 600 Black Belts, 2,500 Green Belts and 18,000 Yellow Belts enrolled or completed trained in DMAIC (Define, Measure, Analyze, Improve and Control) techniques and methods.[v] As was done in the Leadership Through Quality deployment back in the mid 1980's, multiple levels of management were also trained to help create the right environment for success and to educate them on their critical roles.

As we moved through our first year of Xerox's DMAIC Lean Six Sigma deployment, belt candidates and sponsoring managers realized that in many cases that work processes were not documented or those in place were so broken that they were not worth "fixing." Though belt candidates leading these types of projects attempted to utilize the DMAIC tools and methods, they quickly found that the process was not very efficient or effective in those situations and that another roadmap with incremental tools were necessary to meet these challenging projects. Enter DMEDI (or Define, Measure, Explore, Develop and Implement) and Design for Lean Six Sigma for Processes (see Figure 1.2).[vi] If you looking at process side of the roadmap, the first question is does the

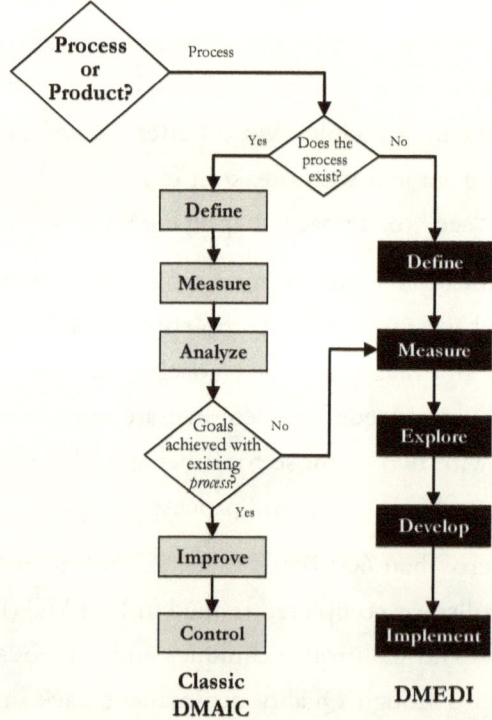

Figure 1.2: Process DMAIC and DMEDI Roadmap

process exist? If yes, then one would follow the DMAIC process through the Analyze phase. At that point, the question is asked can the overall improvement goals be met through the proposed process changes. If yes, then one would proceed through the DMAIC process. If the answer is no, then one would exit DMAIC and start on the DMEDI roadmap to redesign the process to yield the desired results. Though DMAIC and DMEDI share many of the same tools and methods, DMEDI offered belt candidates not only a different roadmap but also incremental tools such as Quality Functional Deployment (or QFD) to better translate the Voice of the Customer, innovation tools for "thinking out of the box", concept selection tools and an introduction to Monte Carlo simulation techniques. This DMEDI curriculum was initially intended to provide Black Belt candidates with incremental tools and methods so that when faced with projects where little or no processes existed, they could "design it right the first time." Though the overall roadmap, framework and content could have been applied to the product design community, we felt the original DMEDI content fell a bit short of what the targeted community needed as it related to Design of Experiments, transfer functions and other product design-related tools. So, teams set off to assess and select the roadmap and content for the Design for Lean Six Sigma Product curriculum.

---

[i] Malcolm Baldrige National Quality Award 1989 Winner document;
http://www.quality.nist.gov/Xerox_89.htm

[ii] Johan Olsson; *The Xerox Corporation: a Case Study*,
http://www.geocities.com/TimesSquare/1848/xerox.html

[iii] *Evolution of Quality at Xerox*,
http://www.xerox.com/downloads/usa/en/n/nr_XeroxLeanSixSigma_2004May.pdf, May, 2004

[iv] http://www.belbin.com/index.htm

[v] Norman Fowler, Nabil Abu Gharbieh, George Maszle, Gilbreath Zealey, "*Lessons learned in the transition from Xerox Lean Six Sigma DMAIC to Design for Lean Six Sigma (DfLSS)*", IQPC 7th Annual DFSS Conference, April 21, 2005.

[vi] Norman Fowler, Nabil Abu Gharbieh, George Maszle, Gilbreath Zealey, "*Lessons learned in the transition from Xerox Lean Six Sigma DMAIC to Design for Lean Six Sigma (DfLSS)*", IQPC 7th Annual DFSS Conference, April 21, 2005.

Chapter 2 Setting the Stage

Establishing the principles and infrastructure necessary for a successful Design for Lean Six Sigma deployment

Toward the end of 2003, there were several initiatives underway that culminated in what now is the Xerox Design for Lean Six Sigma-Product initiative. In mid to late, 2003 a Define, Measure and Analyze (or DMA) project was initiated to assess Xerox development, engineering and product delivery productivity. This initiative was critical for Xerox as competition and the overall marketplace were driving an accelerated rate of new product introductions, offices were migrating to digital multifunction products and color enabled products were beginning to take hold in the work environments around the world. As a company, Xerox was just beginning to turn the financial corner. To meet the growing product demands of our customers and marketplace without adding substantial debt, we needed to look within to drive overall product delivery productivity. The belief was that this productivity would free up resources to attack new markets while retaining support for our core products.

Keys to Success

Design for Lean Six Sigma alone is not a "silver bullet." One must also attack organizational, cultural and other issues to ensure true efficient, effective, and predictable product delivery.

Sponsored by the President of Business Group Operations (Xerox's product delivery organization), this DMA Lean Six Sigma project was aimed at improving the overall product cycle time through the minimization and/or elimination of design-related rework. Breaking it down to a Lean Six Sigma expression $Y=f(x)$ (where the output "Y" is a function of various "x's"), "Y" was considered product delivery rework and the team was interested in identifying the various factors "x" driving the rework. Those "x's" could then be the focal point for other full fledged DMAIC or DMEDI projects or attacked through other means. Through internal interviews, process mapping, benchmarking and other processes and tools, the team was able to identify key drivers to Xerox's product delivery rework. Some directly related to items that were being targeted by the DfLSS initiative such as workforce competencies and requirements management. Others involved a range of cultural and organizational issues outside the Design for Lean Six Sigma scope. This project was critical to getting "traction" for the DfLSS initiative as it documented many of the challenges and issues we had in our product delivery community and pointed to many that could be overcome with Design for Lean Six Sigma tools, methods and discipline.

In parallel with all the other DfLSS-related activities, there was a cross functional team commissioned to look at Systems Engineering practices, skills and competencies. This team took in information from internal sources as well as industry consortiums (e.g. International Council on Systems Engineering or INCOSE) and universities worldwide. This initiative was important as it helped Xerox create a clearer picture of Systems Engineering and the general skills required by our engineering community. The other essential element of this work was that it was accomplished cross functionally with a significant portion of the team from the engineering and research Divisions. The cross-functional nature ensured that all groups were

Keys to Success

By involving the design teams in the DfLSS development you increase the probability of the community accepting the solution.

represented and though it was lead by the centralized Xerox Engineering Center, the actual design community felt they had a significant ownership in the initiative. This involvement by the design community was critical not only for this Systems Engineering initiative, but also for Design for Lean Six Sigma in general. This will be discussed in great detail later. The last Design for Lean Six Sigma related activity was a Massachusetts Institute of Technology study conducted to better understand why past product delivery oriented change initiatives (such as Engineering Excellence) did not "stick" at Xerox. We leveraged several lessons learned from that study to help Design for Lean Six Sigma sustainability and minimize the risk of having to repeat this initiative in another ten years.

As Xerox started our journey toward Design for Lean Six Sigma, there were three individuals and organizations that played a role in the development of the initiative. One of these three key figures was Business Group Operation's Lean Six Sigma Deployment Manager. Since all the design and engineering was performed in this organization, she played a key leadership role and represented the product delivery professionals. The second key leader was the Vice President of the Xerox Engineering Center and Chief Engineer for Xerox. The Xerox Engineering Center was the process owner of both the Xerox Time To Market product delivery process and the overall, high level engineering processes and methods. The third key figure was the Xerox Lean Six Sigma initiative leader.

Early on, a small Design for Lean Six Sigma core team began to interview internal design and engineering leaders, benchmark various external companies on their experiences in DfLSS and assess potential vendor partners to support Xerox's initiative. Some great work was done sifting through all this information and beginning to solidify what Design for Lean Six Sigma meant to Xerox. At this point, we needed a different structure to help drive not only the DfLSS program development, but also the overall program acceptance and ownership by the product delivery organizations.

Establishing DfLSS Launch Team and Principles

To help drive Design for Lean Six Sigma overall direction, a cross organizational and cross functional team known as the "DfLSS Launch Team" was formed. The Launch Team was chaired by Vice President of the Xerox Engineering Center and Vice President of the Corporate Lean Six Sigma Office as they owned the Xerox product delivery processes and Lean Six Sigma initiatives respectively. Other key players on the DfLSS Launch Team were DfLSS Deployment Managers from each technology, design and product delivery organization within Xerox. These Deployment Managers played a key role early on by in bringing in the Voice of the Customer as well as disseminating out important DfLSS messages to the design community. The Launch Team also included the "DfLSS Troika" of Heidi Grenek, Eduardo Bascaran and me. Together, the three of us (with others' support) took over the day to day program development responsibilities. Also participating on the DfLSS Launch Team were the leaders of the three DfLSS initiatives: Electromechanical, Software and Inbound Marketing. These initiative leaders directed the cross-functional and cross-organizational teams established to define their respective DfLSS learning objectives, course content and best practice area descriptions. Heidi played double duty leading the Electromechanical DfLSS Team and the DfLSS initiative as part of the Troika. Various other staff members of both the Xerox Engineering Center and Corporate Lean Six Sigma Office also participated on the DfLSS Launch Team.

With the Launch Team members in place, we then clarified roles and responsibilities to efficiently and thoroughly execute on all components of our deployment while minimizing wasteful overlapping responsibilities. To help this discussion, we mapped out the various steps necessary for a successful DfLSS deployment, drew some boundaries around those functions and built a RACI (Responsible, Accountable, Consulted and Informed) chart to document roles and responsibilities. In general, the working relationships were set up so that the Xerox Engineering Center would own the development of the training specifications (e.g. the content, key learning objectives, etc.) and the Corporate Lean Six Sigma Staff would take the leadership in identifying potential partners for training, coaching and etc. and deploy DfLSS using the existing Lean Six Sigma infrastructure. This proved to be an important step as it set the appropriate

Keys to Success

A RACI diagram is critical with cross-functional teams as it defines and documents roles and responsibilities as well as reduces chance of having political issues.

expectations for each group and minimized the often endless debate on who's doing what. As a group, the DfLSS Launch Team met weekly to review DfLSS program progress, make key policy decisions and to ensure each participating organization was aligned.

One of the DfLSS Launch Team's first initiatives was to develop a set of high level Design for Lean Six Sigma guiding principles that we could build the program around and fall back on when various issues or concerns arose. The ten starting DfLSS principles were as follows:

1. **That Design for Lean Six Sigma would be an integral part of Xerox's Lean Six Sigma deployment.** This principle was important for several reasons. First, we wanted to be sure that both the DMAIC and DfLSS were considered equally important by the entire Xerox community. We did not want to get into the non-value added discussions like "my DfLSS Green Belt is better than

Keys to Success

Having the high level DfLSS principles upfront gave us a foundation to judge our progress, fall back on when there was conflict and to test new ideas.

your DMAIC Green Belt!" Second, we wanted to leverage as much as the existing Lean Six Sigma infrastructure as we could as we rolled DfLSS out to the development and design-oriented organizations. This would minimize resource duplication and keep the overall infrastructure costs to a minimum. We did not want to put an added burden to Xerox or our Lean Six Sigma deployment by staffing up a significant number of DfLSS-only incremental resources. Finally, we decided to add the word "Lean" in our title, bucking what might be considered an industry trend of using Design for Six Sigma. This was done because we were considering the integration of Lean and DMAIC content and principles in the Design for Lean Six Sigma training and to deliver the message that the program was part of the overall corporate Lean Six Sigma imitative.

2. **Operation leaders will be engaged in the process and will integrate DfLSS into their daily business operations.**

3. **Operation management is accountable for specific application of tools and methods to their deliverables inline with business priorities and sound DfLSS practices.** Sometimes in life and in one's career, it is better to be lucky than it is to be good. When we developed and instituted these two principles, I am sure we were both a little bit lucky and good. With the decentralized nature of the Xerox research, design and development organizations, it was clear that it would be difficult to implement and lead this initiative from a centralized staff function. If the Design for Lean Six Sigma initiative was going to be successful, the research, design and development groups ultimately needed to actively participate and take ownership for this program. By engaging the design and development operations from the beginning and involving them in the development of the training objectives, content and other program decisions, it helped gain buy-in for what we were doing in the program's development and

ultimately transfer the DfLSS program ownership to the design-oriented leaders and community.

4. **Consistent with Lean Six Sigma, business impact will be measured and quantified consistent with Lean Six Sigma with benefits demonstrated through improvements in existing Operations' quality, cost and delivery metrics.**

5. **Common in-process metrics will be developed and implemented to assess the DfLSS implementation across the business groups.** The two principles above dealt with metrics and how to measure the success of the Design for Lean Six Sigma program. The first principle was built around how the Corporation would measure the impact of DfLSS methods. Almost from the beginning, the senior technology, design and product delivery leaders felt strongly that it was not necessary to measure the benefits of Design for Lean Six Sigma projects. Here DfLSS project was defined a little different from the classic DMAIC project. As mentioned before, Xerox DMAIC Black Belts are full time dedicated positions. Therefore a significant part of their daily responsibilities was delivering DMAIC projects and their associated results. Because Black Belt led DMAIC projects were identified and selected based on their Division's highest business priorities, there was no guarantee that Black Belts would be assigned projects from their previous specific work groups.

The Design for Lean Six Sigma framework was a bit different. Design for Lean Six Sigma Green Belts and Black Belts were full time product development professionals first and foremost. Our intent from the beginning was making Design for Lean Six Sigma the way product delivery professionals worked and not having it perceived as being incremental to their job responsibilities. The design community and their management were already facing resource constraints and accelerated delivery expectations, so any perceived incremental burdens on the design and technology organizations would not have been easily accepted. In Design for Lean Six Sigma, "projects" were generated around engineer's regular deliverables executed using DfLSS methods, tools and best practices with support from a Master Black Belt coach. In this way, the "projects" were a net benefit to employees (e.g. added help, etc.) instead of being perceived as incremental work.

Why did senior management and others not want to directly measure the impact of DfLSS projects? There were several reasons. First, given the ground work done early on with senior management, many already believed that DfLSS was important and was critical to overall engineering productivity. Therefore, we didn't need a database of projects or counting of benefits to convince them of the power nor the benefits of DfLSS. Second, given the demands on the business, senior management did not want to divert engineers' attention away from solving design-related problems and delivering robust products by having engineers calculating economic savings. This was especially true if the savings were predominately cost avoidances versus cost savings that easily fall to the Corporation's bottom line. Third, cost avoidances (such as potential savings if we had done things business as usual instead of using DfLSS) are usually filled with assumptions that can cause endless, non-value added debate on their relevancy and can distract people from the tasks at hand. There were also concerns expressed by the various organizations how to "divide up" the cost avoidance savings when multiple groups were involved in the solution. Again, this seemed to add little overall value and ultimately would have yielded extended wasteful debates and activities. Finally, given the complexity of the office equipment and the interdependencies between components, modules and subsystems, even a wildly successful individual component-based project may result in very little impact on the overall delivery of the entire product. So rather than spending time quantifying individual projects, we instead celebrated the engineers' accomplishments at internal conferences, senior management meetings, and in publications as well as with our customers. That was extremely important in the initial stages of Design for Lean Six Sigma deployment to demonstrate to people "on the fence" the power of the these methods and tools.

The last thing that product development teams needed was a whole new set of success metrics to track. By using the existing product metrics we could demonstrate how these Design for Lean Six Sigma tools and methods could be integrated into the existing framework without major overhaul of the development process. It also helped reduce the "flavor of the month" mentality as there were not a whole new set of things to measure, track and report on that were not consistent with the way the development teams worked.

While the above dealt with results metrics, there we still needed to come up with a set of in-process metrics to ensure our deployment was pervasive and sustainable. It was agreed up front that a team would work together to develop a common set of these in-process metrics so we could get a sense of how each team, unit and Division were doing on their respective deployments.

6. **All new programs entering the product development process will apply Design for Lean Six Sigma from the beginning.** This principle was put in place to help minimize one common issue seen in other wide spread initiative deployments: managers attempting to opt out of deployment. Typical comments included "this does not pertain to my program" or "that it may be good, but I cannot afford to implement it now." Given the pressures placed on the Divisions to deliver, product development teams could not afford *not* to implement Design for Lean Six Sigma as soon as possible.

7. **The application of Design for Lean Six Sigma concepts and tools will align with existing engineering practices to robustly meet the product development process phase gate deliverables.** This principle was intended to deal with a common question the deployment teams got early on: does Design for Lean Six Sigma replace the Xerox Time To Market product delivery process? The answer was no. In reality, DfLSS augmented the product delivery process and it took a good number of very talented people to articulate the answer in a way that design teams could resonate with. The specifics associated with the integration and synergy of Design for Lean Six Sigma and a product delivery process will be discussed in greater detail later.

8. **Business Operations will deploy and train resources in defined roles using consistent training.** This principle was borrowed from our DMAIC deployment. It was intended to say that each business operation would assign the appropriate resources to make the Design for Lean Six Sigma deployment successful. That included Deployment Managers as well as Green and Black Belts. The principle also supported the fact that Xerox would have one common set of training paths, with a common set of vendor partners teaching from a standard set of materials. This ensured we could get the pervasiveness across Divisions, "speak one language" and use a common set of tools.

9. **Design for Lean Six Sigma Master Black Belt, Black Belt and Green Belt certifications will be achieved through demonstration of the required skills and competencies.** As we began to develop the training and certification architecture, this principle became extremely important. Important because it formed the basis for what many DfLSS professionals believe are unique certification requirements. This will be discussed in greater detail later. This principle also helped overcome a failure mode we had seen in other similar deployments where simply going to class

was sufficient to "pass" and get credit for a training class. This statement clearly indicates that certifications will be based on demonstration of the competencies within the workplace and on the day to day activities of product delivery professionals.

10. **The full value chain (within and across organizations) responsible for the delivery of all products/programs will be trained to the appropriate level.** The final principle had two key elements to it. First, that the entire product delivery value chain would be trained. This included inbound marketing, pure research to product development and manufacturing. If Design for Lean Six Sigma was to become the "way we work" then everyone in that value chain had to be speaking the same language and be competent in using the DfLSS methods and tools. The second key element to that sentence was "appropriate." This gave each business operation the ability to look within their respective organization and identify which people to train at each competency level based on their current and future roles (Green Belt, Black Belt, etc.). Once a Division indicated that all of their Design Managers would be required to be Design for Lean Six Sigma Black Belts, it sent clear message and set the appropriate expectation that this initiative was important for an engineer's career growth.

We set a target that 100 percent of the eligible research, development and engineering population would be trained to at least a Green Belt level. At the time, that assumption was that roughly 4000 researchers, engineers and the other related product delivery professionals would be trained over approximately five years. Once we got to steady state, roughly 25 percent of the population (or roughly 1000) would be DfLSS Black Belts.

Chronologically, the Electromechanical program was the first Design for Lean Six Sigma initiative that was developed. This was due to the fact people were already familiar with the concepts from Engineering

Excellence initiative and there were existing "pockets of excellence" already utilizing many of the DfLSS tools and techniques. The cross functional Systems Engineering team also had been working on similar content for roughly a year. Given the synergy of goals and the team's existing representation, the Systems Engineering Team morphed into the DfLSS Electromechanical Core Team. The Core Team was charged with determining the Electromechanical Design for Lean Six Sigma training content. However, because it was the first DfLSS initiative, additional work needed to be done in parallel to define things such as certification criteria, Design for Lean Six Sigma Belt definitions and coaching just to name a few. That additional work was chartered for the DfLSS Troika. So, in conjunction to the Electromechanical Core Team building the training content, the DfLSS Troika was working the infrastructure elements so that both could be accomplished in a timely manner.

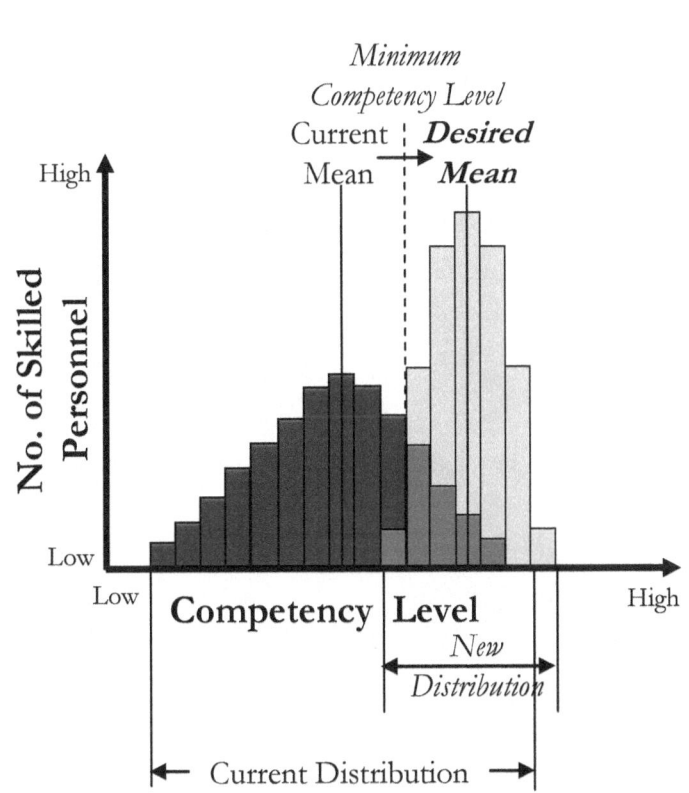

The training goal of 100 percent of the eligible population trained was intended to raise the competency level of the entire product delivery community. The focus was to raise the majority of the population above the minimum DfLSS competency level (shifting the overall competency level mean to the right) and narrowing the overall competency distribution. Unlike our DMAIC deployment, we felt *everyone* needed to be trained to at least a Green Belt level to make DfLSS the "way we work" and sustainable over time.

**Figure 2.1: Raising the Product Delivery
Community Competency Level**

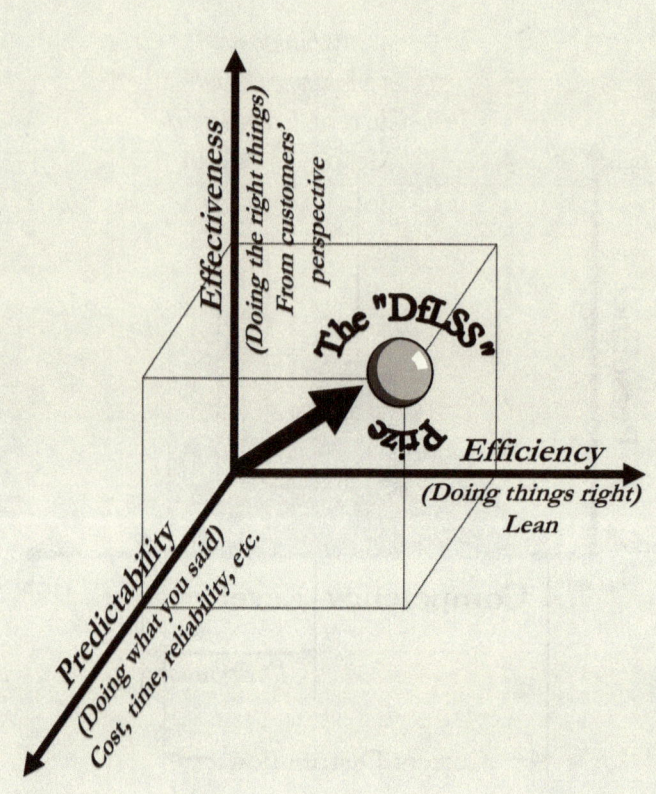

One of our Design for Lean Six Sigma program goals was to ensure the curriculum and overall deployment would enable certified belts and design teams to optimize all three product delivery dimensions: efficiency, effectiveness and predictability. Efficiency is defined as "doing things right" in a Lean, waste-free manner. Effectiveness is "doing the right things" from our customers' perspective. Predictability is "doing what you said" by delivering on time, on budget and to your customers' requirements. Delivering on all three dimensions will yield the "DfLSS Prize."

Figure 2.2: The "DfLSS Prize Matrix"

Chapter 3

Developing and Delivering the Program

How we developed the Design for Lean Six Sigma curriculum, certification process and drove it into the design community

As we set out to develop the Design for Lean Six Sigma Electromechanical curriculum, we made a conscious decision to ensure that there was not a significant perceived difference by Xerox employees between the DMAIC Lean Six Sigma and Design for Lean Six Sigma programs. By that, we wanted to have the basic training and certification structure and requirements viewed as similar in complexity and difficulty. This was because we did not establish nor encourage the non-value added debate on which of the two programs was more difficult or important. Both programs were important to Xerox's success and we wanted them to be on equal footing. Therefore a tenant of our curriculum development was that we needed to be sensitive to having both DMAIC and DfLSS certification as equivalent in both difficulty and importance. We also felt it was important to leverage the lessons learned from the Xerox DMAIC Lean Six Sigma curriculum design. There were some items in the DMAIC curriculum and deployment that worked for the Xerox product development community that we felt we could leverage and a few items that did not make sense to the DfLSS program that we had to find a unique set of solutions for.

Establishing a Building Block Belt Structure

One lesson learned from the Xerox DMAIC deployment was to have the Design for Lean Six Sigma Black Belt curriculum "build on" the Green Belt curriculum versus having two distinct programs. As we started the DfLSS curriculum design we were several years into the DMAIC deployment and started to have individuals who had completed their Green Belt training and certification become candidates for DMAIC Black Belts. As they entered the Black Belt program they found that much of the Black Belt content was the same as the Green Belt content. After teaching the DMAIC Green Belts about the identification and elimination of waste, we turned around and taught them the same material over again. This became an issue for many of the Black Belt candidates as they rightfully saw the repeat of material they had already mastered as waste. Now, it's not to say the initial approach Xerox took was bad. We needed one percent of our population trained and operating as Black Belts to "prime the DMAIC pump" and ensure the early success of our program. At the start of the Xerox Lean Six Sigma deployment, we needed to have separate DMAIC Green Belt and Black Belt programs. However, after several years in, we saw the overlap as an element that needed to be changed for Design for Lean Six Sigma.

Keys to Success

Do not be afraid to reexamine and change fundamental elements of your deployment if a better is found.

By having the DfLSS Black Belt build on the Green Belt experience, you also enabled people to take the Black Belt classes and meet the requirements over a period of time. This was important given we did not want to give the perception that the DfLSS program was going to burdened already taxed engineers. By having the Black Belts become practicing Green Belts first, we had a chance to see how the Green Belt has mastered the skills and competencies before committing them to the Black Belt program. After observing the success of the DfLSS Black Belt building on the Green Belt, the Xerox Corporate Lean Six Sigma Office decided to move toward changing the DMAIC model to match the DfLSS building block structure.

As we started to build the Design for Lean Six Sigma program structure, we began with the graphical representation of the competency framework displayed in Figure 3.1.[i] The framework was a graph of the number of tools and methods a belt candidate would be expected to master versus the depth of tools and methods knowledge demonstrated by that belt candidate. Starting with one of the DfLSS basic principles described in Chapter Two, the assumption was that 100 percent of the eligible product delivery professional population would be Green Belts; it led to the graphic displayed in Figure 3.2. There would be a set number of tools and methods Green Belts would have to master to a sufficient depth. From a terminology perspective, we gave this group the title of "practioner." As practioners, these candidates would be asked to competently perform a series of DfLSS activities and use related methods on their own.

Using the same framework, we continued and defined the DfLSS Black Belt configuration as illustrated in Figure 3.3. As one might expect, the Black Belt content included a greater number of tools and methods to be mastered at an overall greater depth. As mentioned previously, our initial estimate was that 25 percent of the product delivery professional population would ultimately attain the DfLSS Black Belt competency level when we reached steady state. We referred to these Black Belts as "specialists" or individuals who have command of the subject matter, can guide other practioners and can apply knowledge to complex problems.

At the start, we did not have a very much discussion on the structure of the Master Black Belt curriculum. We were more interested in getting not only the Green Belt and Black Belt content established but in starting to work on other disciplines such as DfLSS Software and Inbound Marketing. Over time, the Master Black Belt model began to evolve.

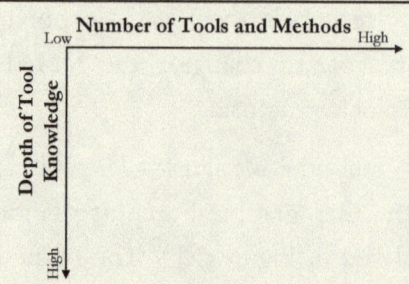

Figure 3.1: DfLSS Competency Framework

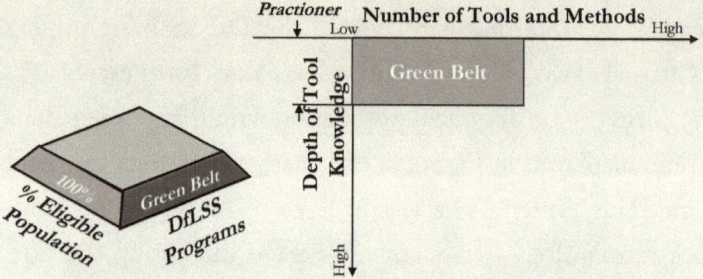

Figure 3.2: Green Belt Competency Configuration

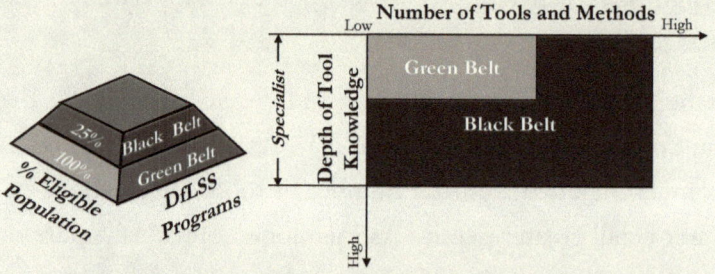

Figure 3.3: Black Belt Competency Configuration

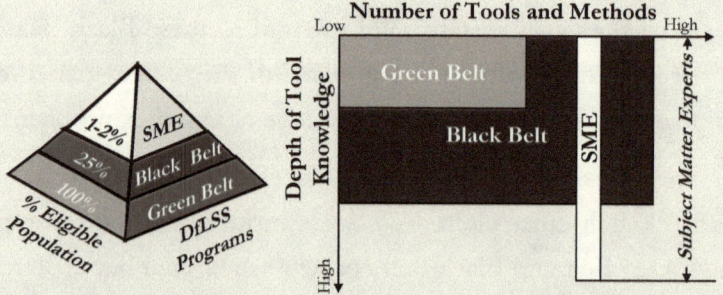

Figure 3.4: Subject Matter Expert Competency Configuration

Master Black Belt candidates were highly skilled Black Belts that were given full time assignments to support Deployment Managers drive DfLSS into their organizations, provide organization leaders with coaching and lead the integration of highly sophisticated development projects.

We also added one other competency definition: Subject Matter Expert or SME which is illustrated in Figure 3.4. The SMEs were individuals who may not be initially DfLSS belts, but have deep knowledge on a narrow set of DfLSS tools and methods.

Subject Matter Experts typically would be called in on highly complex, cross organizational issues that required their in-depth skills. This SME designation also gave recognition for those internal resources that had

attained technical reputation and respect both internally and externally to the company. In many cases, these individuals have some fairly significant say in what is accepted and not accepted with the technical community. This designation helped break any perceived notion that the DfLSS program was going to replace their positions in their respective

Keys to Success

Find and leverage internal DfLSS Subject Matter Experts as they can be key opinion leaders, support the development of the program and you do not want them to perceive DfLSS as a threat to their position within their respective organization.

organizations and helped pull them into the discussions around what skills and requirements would be necessary for certification. By using this designation, we helped minimize what would have been a significant barrier to our deployment across each Division and the company.

Developing the Design for Lean Six Sigma Program Content Structure

To build a new competency-based Design for Lean Six Sigma program model, we needed content and a methodology that would support

35

certification. The starting point for this content framework was the previously mentioned cross organizational team that was working independently on Systems Engineering best practices. The team had worked for over a year to identify and converge on a set of recognized System Engineering best practices. This was done by benchmarking various companies and universities as well as industrial associations such as International Council on Systems Engineering (INCOSE). Through their work, the team converged on thirteen System Engineering best practices which can be found in Table 3.1 numbered 1 through 12. The remaining set of three competencies will be discussed shortly. We liked the Systems Engineering framework as it included all aspects of product development and delivery from start to finish. That was important as not every Xerox engineer was doing the exact same job function nor was every new product program at the same point in the product delivery process at any given time. At the Systems Engineering level, we found almost every electromechanical-based product delivery professional could also find an appropriate link between a significant portion of the best practices and their current job responsibilities.

Keys to Success
Consider using benchmark work done by various organizations in the field of interest as it can bring credibility and allows you to use precious intellectual resources on how to the information may apply to your organization.

After some analysis and debate, we added three competencies to the standard Systems Engineering list we felt were critical to the success of the overall program: (1) DfLSS software tools, (2) DfLSS overview and burning platform and (3) coaching. The intent of adding the DfLSS software tools was to ensure that each individual could master the set of supporting software tools that we ultimately would converge on. This would give each engineer that common language to talk and a common

Table 3.1: DfLSS Best Practices Areas

1. *	Project Management
2. *	Voice of the Customer Gathering and Product Requirements Generation
3. *	Concept Generation and Selection
4. *	System Design
5. *	Requirements Engineering
6. *	Statistical Tool Box
7. *	Analytical Modeling & Simulation
8a.*	Design of Experiments for Empirical Modeling and Simulation
8b.*	Robust Design & Optimization Methods
9. *	Tolerancing and Specifications
10. *	Reliability Methods
11. *	Design and Process Capability
12. *	"Design for X" (e.g. service, regulatory, release management, reuse, manufacturing, etc.)
13.	DfLSS Software Tools
14.	DfLSS Overview and Burning Platform
15.	Coaching

*The initial set of System Engineering competencies

set of tools that would allow the efficient and effective collaboration. We also thought it was critical for each student to understand *why* DfLSS was being adopted. To that end, we developed the Xerox DfLSS "burning platform." The term burning platform within the context of business can be explained by Ken Embley, Center for Public Policy &

Administration Organizational Development Consultant, through the following story:

> "A man working on a North Sea oil platform is awakened suddenly one night by an explosion. As the worker made his way to the edge of the platform with flames all around him, he decided to jump off the platform and into the sea. He did this even though jumping was a risky option due to the 150 foot drop to the water that was filled with burning oil and debris and not to mention the chilly 40 °F water that would kill him due to exposure in 15 minutes. Luckily, the man survived the jump and was brought to safety by a rescue boat. When asked why he jumped, the response was "better probably death than certain death." The point here is that the "burning platform" caused a radical change in his behavior." [ii]

Ken Embley went on to say that "your ability to identify "burning" change issues and separate them from the routine challenges of the day will have a great effect on a stakeholder's willingness to accept change and adapt to a new way of thinking about the important issue." We needed to create a presentation that helped identify the critical challenges facing Xerox's design and development organizations, highlight the compelling reasons for a sense of urgency and insure that everyone hears and understands why Xerox is embracing Design for Lean Six Sigma. The hope was that this burning platform would be one of the catalysts necessary to accelerate acceptance and pervasiveness of the DfLSS solution path.

Keys to Success

The DfLSS Burning Platform was important as it not only communicated to the design community "what is DfLSS" but also "why we needed it."

The last of the three skills that were added was coaching. It has been my observation over the last several years that many DMAIC and DfLSS belt candidates found true coaching difficult and were less proficient at it than either managing projects and/or people. Picking up from our DMAIC deployment experiences, we knew that coaching would be critical to the long term success of the DfLSS deployment. In fact, it proved to be even more important as we moved along in our development and deployment than we initially realized.

Looking back on successful and failed attempts to deploy similar types of initiatives, those that included coaching after the training and required demonstration of the skills tended to be more successful. Just attending and participating in a class does not ensure that students going back to their work environment would apply the newly acquired skills or have the support to reinforce their learning. In fact, they were more likely to be more influenced by their existing work place group norms and fall back into existing and less productive work processes and behaviors. To ensure a degree of "stickiness" to the program, we knew we had to have coaching and routine touch points with the students over an extended period of time to help reinforce the desired skills and to help them resist the pressures of their group norms. The post-class demonstration of skills was intended to reinforce the general tools and methods sets, get another cycle of learning under the student's belt and demonstrate they could apply the tools in their own work environment. The hypothesis was that the majority of the DfLSS belt candidates would not really internalize the new methods and tools unless they could apply them under the normal stresses and demands of their work environments. Right from the beginning, our organizational construct

Keys to Success

Having belt candidates demonstrate applying the DfLSS tools in their own work environment (versus in a "safe" class room) made sure the candidates mastered the skills with all the normal daily distractions, gave them another cycle of learning and increased the chance the skills would be internalized.

model was that key product design leaders would be Design for Lean Six Sigma Black Belts with a majority of their subordinates being Green Belts. This construct created a natural coaching situation. For many belt candidates, coaching skills did not come naturally. So we intended to add a training program to help those belt candidates become better coaches for their managers, peers and subordinates.

Developing the Design for Lean Six Sigma Certification Process

Armed with the full set of DfLSS best practices we still did not have an elegant way of implementing the DfLSS certification process. Again, many other Lean Six Sigma certification requirements include completion of a "project." We started at that point, but quickly realized that this model would actually hurt adoption of the DfLSS principles, not support it in our situation. This was predominately due to the fact that Xerox product delivery time was typically measured in years, not months or weeks like other DMAIC projects. We felt that no organization or individual could sustain that level of enthusiasm or

Keys to Success

Certification completion cycle time was important: too quick and it can be perceived as too easy; too long candidates can loose momentum and interest.

momentum for the several years necessary to launch a new product and get their DfLSS certification. Therefore, we needed to develop a different model that allowed a reasonable cycle time to earn certification. This proved to be more of a struggle than one might imagine. We brainstormed several different options, but none seem to capture what we really needed or that would work in Xerox's environment.

Breakthroughs sometime result from a structured process, effective brainstorming and use of other innovation techniques. Other times, they do not. Back in early 2005, I was sick in bed with a severe cold. I was in a funky state of mind thinking about work, when all of a sudden I came up with the idea of creating a matrix using the engineering best practices down the page and an existing Xerox skills rating system across the top. This basic skills rating scale had been used extensively by Xerox in the past and was based on a proficiency scale with "1" being awareness, "3" being a practioner and "5" being a subject matter expert or master.

These five levels of proficiency were later redefined to better align to the DfLSS certification structure. Awareness (level 1) was an entry level of performance, able to describe basic principles and benefits. Level 2 was defined as "candidate" in that individuals could perform some fundamental operations, but required guidance and support for a majority of the DfLSS methods and processes. The practioner level (level 3) was defined as the ability to competently perform, on one's own, a particular skill or set of skills. The level 4 designation was defined as

Keys to Success

Leveraging existing material or other artifacts (e.g. skills rating system) can tie a new initiative to the past, help minimize the "new" content and reduce peoples' change anxiety.

"expert" with a command of the subject matter and the ability to guide other practioners in applying the tools and methods. Finally, the subject matter expert or master (level 5) has expert command of set of methods and tools, coaches other candidates on the job and teaches classes on their area of mastery. Level 5 Masters also can synthesize, analyze and solve complex problems in new situations and may be an externally recognized expert in the field.

With this basic matrix in hand (Design for Lean Six Sigma competencies listed down the page and competency levels across the top), I envisioned that the intersection of a best practice area and competency level would have a written definition of what was required to be at the level (from awareness to master). With this matrix completely populated with descriptors, all we had to do was to agree what competencies and what levels would be required for various belt certification levels. I got so excited, I dragged myself out of bed to my home office and emailed the idea to my "partners in crime", the DfLSS Troika. I was so sick, just that expenditure of energy was enough to put me back into bed for hours. By the time I returned to work the next day, we had realized that we stumbled onto the certification framework we were looking for.

Keys to Success

Sometimes being lucky is better than being good, but you can not count on being lucky all the time!

Given the innovative people we had on this initiative, it did not take long to build on the brainstormed certification framework concept. We quickly converged on a set of simple definition principles and divided each of the best practice rows to team members who had the responsibility to draft a set of competency definitions. Through a series of meetings, we plowed through each set of competency definitions until resident Subject Matter Experts and team members agreed on each cell's description.

With an agreed upon set of operational definitions for each best practice area and each level of competency in place, we next had to set up some overarching certification principles. For example, we agreed that all level one (awareness) and two (candidate) levels of competency could be demonstrated through "teachbacks." In this context, a teachback refers to the belt candidate teaching back or explaining to their coach in their own words what the skill or methods is, how it's used and how it would apply in the belt's

Keys to Success

In writing the competency level definitions, emphasis was placed on simpler versus complex definitions. If the certification matrix gets too big and complicated it will not be read or used. You are better off working with coaches to ensure good operational definitions behind the scenes on what is needed to meet requirements than having an all encompassing document.

work environment. For competency levels three (practioner) and above, hard evidence of applying the tool into their work environment would be required. Since we already realized that full blown DfLSS projects didn't make sense for Xerox, we converged on the use of "studies." For the purposes of DfLSS certification, a study was an application of a tool or method in a product delivery professional's work environment. Conducting a scouting Design of Experiment (DoE), or a Measurement System Analysis (MSA) or exercising other DfLSS tools within their respective best practice area would be considered a study. This concept was critical as it enabled the desired demonstration of skills within a belt's work environment for certification credit without having candidates wait until the entire product was launched. Unlike many DMAIC projects, DfLSS studies are not special tasks or projects to be completed for certification. For the DfLSS certification, the belt candidate was expected to take DfLSS tools and apply them to their normal, day-to-day assignments or objectives. Again, we were striving to get engineers and other product delivery professionals to apply these techniques to the way they worked and not have them perceived as "something extra to do." Figure 3.5 illustrates the structure of the Design for Lean Six Sigma certification matrix.

We did shamelessly borrow an element from our DMAIC projects by having a DfLSS study charter. The study charter had elements similar to a DMAIC charter such as an objective, high level delivery dates, etc. However, the DfLSS study charter had a much narrower scope as it pertained to utilization of one or very few number of tools. The belt candidate, their manager and their coach were required to sign off on the charter in the

Keys to Success

Having a signed project charter helps ensure all parties (belt candidate, coach and candidate's management) understand and agree on what is to be accomplished, priorities, timing and that available resources are available.

43

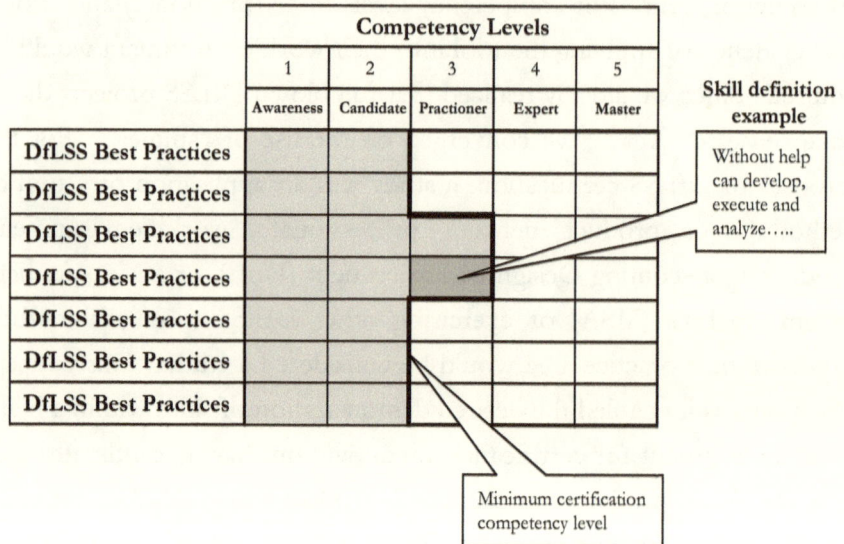

**Figure 3.5: Design for Lean Six Sigma
Certification Matrix Illustration**

beginning. The belt and his/her manager would sign off to ensure that the scope was correct, the timetable agreed to and the resources would be available to execute the study. The signature of the coach was to ensure this would meet the minimum certification requirements for the targeted level of competency before the actual work was initiated. The belt candidate would then execute the study charter and deliver the results. At the end of the study, all three would then sign again to ensure the work was completed (belt candidate and manager) and the competency was successfully demonstrated (belt candidate and coach).

With the certification framework in hand, the next step was to set what collection of best practices and levels of competencies would be required for both DfLSS Green and Black Belts certifications. This actually took a bit longer to work out than we initially had hoped. Given we started with Electromechanical curriculum, we began to look at what type of product delivery professionals would fall into this category. In a company like Xerox, the product delivery professional jobs ranged from the research chemist working on innovation breakthroughs to a manufacturing engineer working on the factory floor and everything in between. As mentioned before, Xerox product delivery times were relatively long. This meant that an engineer in the later phases of a new product development cycle would not have the opportunity to demonstrate tools such as QFD that are typically applied early in the product development cycle. Therefore, we knew our certification process had to have flexibility to be relevant no matter where in the product delivery process the candidate was in.

The one item that we all quickly agreed to was that a practioner level of competency (Level 3) for Design of Experiment (DoE) was a minimum requirement all Green Belt candidates as it was the heart and soul of developing transfer functions and is the cornerstone of DfLSS. The cross functional core team then agreed that each Electromechanical Green belt candidate must choose two other best practice areas for the required practioner-level performance (or Level 3, the ability to utilize DfLSS methods without help) that were consistent with their job function and where they were on their product program delivery. This certification flexibility helped ensure each job function, independent of where they were in the product design cycle, could find and demonstrate at least two other areas to demonstrate competency. A practioner level 3 was also required for the two added skills: DfLSS Software tools (for DoE, Monte Carlo analysis, etc.) and the DfLSS Burning Platform. Each Green Belt candidate needed to demonstrate their mastery of the important analytical software tools as well as how the burning platform impacted their job functions. For all other best practice areas not at level 3 or above, the candidate needed to meet at least level 2 (which we defined as could accomplish the best practice with help) demonstrated through teachbacks. This was required to ensure each candidate had a working knowledge of and internalized the entire set of DfLSS competencies and skills.

The next question the core team grappled with was how would these competencies be assessed? By this time in Xerox's DMAIC Lean Six

Sigma deployment, we had a hundreds of DMAIC Black Belts and Master Black Belts which could be asked to play this coaching role. However, we were concerned of the "opportunity lost" by distracting these Belts from their project work. These highly trained and skilled individuals were providing a better service to Xerox by attacking and solving many of the critical business issues facing the company and eliminating the waste in each operation. Therefore, we concluded the best overall option was to utilize the training consultant's resources for this coaching and certification skill validation.

How much coaching should a DfLSS belt candidate get? To help answer that question, we fell back on one of our principles that the DfLSS and DMAIC programs should be considered equivalent. We were able to get some data from our DMAIC consulting partners and internal coaches how much total time each belt was utilizing in their coaching sessions. Next we documented some DfLSS training and coaching assumptions. These included the following: there would be 25 students in a class or what would be called a "wave". Each training wave would get their own coach for their entire certification process and that certified coaches would be here for a week per month to coach their wave. Accounting for the fact that not each student would be available each coaching session, we concluded that each coaching session could be roughly 90 minutes and still meet the one week of a coach's time. Dividing that into the average total coaching time we got from the DMAIC coaches, we concluded that it would take roughly eight coaching sessions to get through certification. This process was far from being scientific, but it gave us a reasonable starting point.

We also decided the coaching sessions would be set up on a "push" basis. By that, each series of coaching week dates would be set several months in advance. The coaches would send out a schedule of open times and belt candidates would respond by email and fill in the times they could make their coaching appointment. These would be the only coaching and validation sessions offered to each candidate, so we stressed to them that all their competencies needed to be validated within the allotted times and number of coaching sessions.

As far as the time between coaching sessions, we started by making them roughly every 4-6 weeks apart. This was done for several reasons. One was to ensure there was enough time between coaching sessions to ensure supporting work could get done such as setting up and running a Design of Experiment. Second, we wanted to ensure that each belt candidate had regular spaced engagements with a DfLSS expert over an extended period of time. This would help reinforce the new tools, techniques and methods by

Keys to Success

Having study and project examples integrated into the training helps demonstrate these techniques can be used in your work environment and increases the chances of connecting with belt candidates.

having multiple and regular cycles of learning to make Design for Lean Six Sigma a "habit." The more cycles of learning, the greater the probability of making DfLSS stick. We felt this was a critical enabler for a sustained deployment.

There was at least one positive unintended consequence of this coaching model as well. By having the partner Master Black Belt coaching waves of Xerox belt candidates, it accelerated the coaches' knowledge of the xerographic process, key products that Xerox was either developing or improving and most importantly, picking up the Xerox language, terminology and acronyms. Why was this important? When we began Xerox's DMAIC deployment, our consulting partner was very knowledgeable of the statistical tools, but not necessarily of Xerox and how it worked. Without this background, the classroom training examples had to be generic so that people from all disciplines could understand them (e.g. making pizza). Early on, some belt candidates found this frustrating as the instructors could not easily converse in Xerox language and back up their instruction with Xerox examples. I've found that at least at Xerox, that the farther an individual's job is from manufacturing in the value chain, the more student needs to be shown exactly how the tools and methods are applied in their world.

For the DMAIC training initiative, it took six to twelve months before the instructors picked up enough terminology and Xerox examples to make the training "real" for all students. In the DfLSS deployment, since coaching began immediately after the training, the coaches were quickly immersed into Xerox terminology, had the opportunity to see the products students were talking about and were brought up to speed on the technically complex environments that the belt candidates were working in. The coaches, who were also the instructors, then could immediately take those experiences to the class room which gave a much more robust educational experience. Overall, this process took one or two months versus the six to twelve months for the DMAIC deployment. In hindsight, many times you look back on decisions that you made and realize the positive or negative impacts of those decisions. In this case, implementing this coaching model was one decision that had significant positive impact on the DfLSS program's short and long term "stickiness".

Selecting a Partner Consulting Firm

In parallel with the certification methodology development, we also focused on potential consultant firms to form our training partnership. Early on in Xerox's Lean Six Sigma program development, the Xerox Engineering Center and the Lean Six Sigma Deployment Managers for product design-related Divisions led an initiative in Design for Lean Six Sigma. This included conducting the previously mentioned project on design-related rework, benchmarking other successful DfLSS deployments and conducting a consulting firm search and selection process. The selection process included extensive interviews, discussions with their current clients and a set of evaluation criteria against which each candidate partner was judged. The outcome of that selection process yielded a highly qualified initial partner for our DfLSS program. They came highly recommended and had the credentials and track record that gave people confidence in this partnership. Unfortunately for Xerox and this initial consulting partner, there were several things that converged that limited the success of this first engagement.

As in Xerox's DMAIC deployment, we started with training a wave of DfLSS Black Belts. We asked for the "best and brightest" Design for Lean Six Sigma belt candidates just as we did when starting the DMAIC deployment. The first set of DfLSS candidates submitted from each Division was an impressive group of highly respected opinion and organization leaders. The downside of this group was that with their participation came some caveats. First, unlike our DMAIC Black Belt candidates, the DfLSS Black Belt candidates maintained their current job responsibilities and were not full time, dedicated belts. Division leaders also felt they could not give up these essential people for four full weeks of Black Belt training as most were in the middle of delivering critical product programs. So, a compromise was made to break up the training in to two to three days a month spread over several months. In hindsight, the Xerox DfLSS deployment community and the consulting partner should have raised their hands and questioned this decision, but the training moved forward.

What further complicated the issue was that we "did not start at the beginning." By that I mean, the Division leaders also wanted to begin the training out of sequence focusing first on the tools that they felt they could use immediately. This initially seemed somewhat reasonable. However given the interaction between many tools and methods, we found it difficult to effectively teach one topic without bringing in the other related topics. This created confusion in not only the students, but also the instructors. One other issue was that we choose a training location too close to the belt candidates' work environment. In many instances, when there were breaks in the training or for lunch, candidates would leave, go back to their offices and find a crisis or urgent issue that needed to be resolved. This resulted in people moving in and out of the classes which disrupted their learning and their fellow teammates. These factors unfairly and negatively impacted the perception of the consulting partner even though they were only responding to our training requests and guidelines.

Other factors came in to play that impacted the perception of our first DfLSS consulting partner. During the first management training session, we realized that the consulting partner placed a significant emphasis on DfLSS tools and project discipline and a good portion Xerox's design related management was less willing or not ready to accept that level of tool usage and overall process discipline in their product development processes. Unfortunately, the Xerox deployment community underestimated both this significant difference in perspective and how firm both parties held to their relative positions. From the consulting partner perspective, each of their successful deployments had the same disciplined approach. Not all Xerox management had been exposed to the DfLSS tools and methods prior to this training and many were not willing to put their programs at perceived risk by adopting these principles even after their management training. Without management support, the right environment could not be created that would allow those belt candidates to successfully complete their projects or studies. This gap between what the consultant felt needed to be done versus what management was willing to implement created more challenges for the deployment team. The Xerox management perspective on DfLSS triggered a few internal political discussions which tended to add more unwanted "noise" to the overall initiative.

One more contributing factor to the somewhat unenthusiastic response to the consulting partner's teaching style. The consulting partner's mastery of the tools and overall DfLSS process was and still is excellent. Their printed training content was also very good. However, many students found that the instructors' styles were to "mechanical" and not "inspiring" enough for the Xerox culture. The selected consulting partner's style was very effective in companies we talked to, but for the Xerox environment, it just did not seem to be an optimum fit.

Just as we were working the first draft of the certification process, there was internal Xerox pressure to look into other potential consulting partner alternatives. Art Fornari had just returned from a Lean Six Sigma conference and heard Dr. Mark Kiemele, President and Co-founder of Air Academy Associates, present. He was impressed with Mark's messages, philosophies and overall enthusiasm and passion for Lean Six Sigma. After some internal discussions with various stakeholders in the DfLSS deployment, we decided to run a "face-off" between our first consulting partner and Air Academy Associates.

The first face-off was for management training. Since our first consulting partner had already conducted their management training session, we brought Air Academy in for their trial. Luckily, we included a fairly detailed set of course evaluation questions at the first management training session which we repeated at the end of the Air Academy management session to help in comparing "apples to apples." We also worked with the various design-related Divisions to select the right audience for this face-off session. To ensure a consistent assessment, we had a portion of the class who participated in the first management training session sit in on the second. We also

Keys to Success

Having a detailed training class survey gave us feedback on what people liked, did not like and where changes needed to be made. Tracking these results over time gave us important trend data so we could compare within and across classes, training sites, instructors, etc. and take action when it was required.

wanted to get a fresh perspective that was not necessarily biased by the first consulting partner's presentation. To get this, we filled part of the Air Academy class with a new group of managers who had not been exposed to DfLSS or the first consulting partner before. Each manager was hand picked to ensure that key organizations and functions would contribute to the assessment. Finally, members of the deployment and Corporate Lean Six Sigma Office were asked to attend to make sure that they understood the management training content and experience Mark's presentation style. Once both management training sessions were complete, the course evaluation data was analyzed, but kept confidential until the next phase of the assessment process.

I was asked to lead a cross-functional team to review the class feedback data and recommend to the DfLSS Core Team which consulting firm we should use for our management training. We knew this decision was an important one in that we had just one more opportunity to "get this right" as our design community was losing some patience. We also realized that if we were ever going to be successful getting a pervasive and a sustainable DfLSS deployment, we needed much more involvement and overall process ownership from each of the design and product delivery based organizations. The more it became "their" process and they had a hand in developing and agreeing on the program elements, the better our chances for an overall successful deployment. So I pulled a small team of opinion leaders, Deployment Managers and functional managers together to review and make the sourcing recommendation to the full DfLSS Launch Team. As one might expect, there were a number of strong opinions and emotions tied up in this decision. I concluded the best path to take was to use the DfLSS tools and methods we had learned and put them to work to help remove some of the emotions involved in this decision. By doing this, hopefully we could focus more on the class feedback data and facts than falling prey to an emotional decision. I decided to use a modified Delphi technique to solicit inputs and build a set of decision criteria as well as a weighted Pugh matrix methodology to sort through a variety of decision criteria and the two consulting partner options.[iii]

Given the team participants were very busy managers, my first engagement was a Delphi-like interaction email versus scheduling multiple face to face meetings. The decision needed to be made in short order, so my first email included the decision meeting date and time as well as a brainstormed list of candidate decision criteria. I asked each member to rank the top eight decision criteria in order of importance and to send back their input as soon as possible. This gave each person the opportunity to do the initial ranking independently and without any influence from others. Borrowing that collectively we were more intelligent than any one of us individually, I summed up everyone's input and separated the most important criteria from those less important. Then I used each criterion's individual score divided by the total score of all the selected criteria to get a percentage value as a weighting factor. Other techniques like Analytic Hierarchy Process (AHP) could have been used to develop the relative weights, but the time deadline and the difficulty of getting these managers together at one time to work through the analysis made it almost impossible.

Keys to Success

When faced with tough decisions, use the Lean Six Sigma methods and tools set to help take out some of the emotion. It demonstrates that you can "eat your own cooking" and that the staff is committed to the methods and tools as well.

Prior to the selection meeting, I sent out a second email package that included classes' survey results, the feedback analysis and the relative weight results. The email also included the request that each team member assess if the Air Academy was much worse, worse, the same, better or much better for each criterion than the initial consulting partner and to return their response to me prior to our meeting. This gave us the opportunity for each team member to personally assess both options on their own. As I collected the team members' responses, I was able to get the "sense of the house" or where everyone's positions were before walking into the face-to-face decision meeting.

We started the decision meeting by making sure each participant understood the desired outcome of the meeting (making a training partner recommendation) and reviewed the class feedback statistics to insure everyone was on the same page. Next I showed the results of the weighting work the team had done independently to see if it made sense and represented the relative importance of each criterion. I felt it was important to get the team to agree on the overall process and weights before we dove into their individual ratings. After some discussion and clarification, the team accepted the weighted criteria results. The last document I shared was the first draft of the modified Pugh matrix. Table 3.2 illustrates the framework of that Pugh matrix. Here I had each of the criteria listed down the left hand column, their respective weights in the next column, the baseline initial firm scores (all zero's) and then five other Air Academy rating columns. These five columns were marked "- -", "-", "0", "+" and "++". Using the initial consultant as the baseline, "- -" meant that Air Academy was much worse that the initial consultant's management training, "0" meant both suppliers were the same and "++" meant that Air Academy was much better than the initial consultant's training. In these last five columns, I displayed how many of the team members independently voted for each level of performance rating for each criteria. As a team we went through each

Table 3.2: Management Training Pugh Matrix

			Air	Academy				
			-9	-3	0	+3	+9	
Criteria	Weight	Initial Firm	Much Worse (- -)	Worse (-)	Same (0)	Better (+)	Much Better (++)	Total
		0						
		0						
		0						
	1.00	0						

criterion, one by one, focusing our discussion with those people who voted at the extremes (significantly higher or lower than the balance of the group). Once the discussion was complete, I gave each member the chance to change their vote. This continued until each criterion was discussed and all points of views were considered. With this in hand, I moved to another linked Excel® window that "did the math" and calculated the overall score. The total for each criterion was calculated by taking the number of people who voted for "much worse", multiplying it by minus nine and the weight for that criterion. That calculation continued across the four other ratings and was summed up at the end to get the total. After each criterion total was calculated, the last column was totaled and an overall score was calculated. If the current consulting partner was favored, the overall score would have been negative and conversely, if Air Academy Associates was favored, it would result in a positive score. The overall results were positive and therefore the initial results suggested that Air Academy Associates was favored.

At this point we stepped back and asked ourselves if the outcome made sense. After some conversation, the team agreed one more time with the overall process, the criteria and relative weights and the final outcome to change our consulting partner for the management training to Air Academy Associates. All together, this decision meeting lasted about an hour. This relatively short meeting given the emotional aspects associated with this topic was enabled by the upfront work facilitated by the Delphi process emails and use of one of Design for Lean Six Sigma's most powerful tools, the Pugh Matrix. This recommendation was validated by the entire DfLSS Launch Team, communicated to all partners and implemented immediately.

With the management training decision behind us, the next decision that was made was who would be our lead consulting firm for the Green Belt and Black Belt curriculums. Given the success we had with the management training selection process, we followed the same basic process for deciding the belt program consulting firm. Again, the two candidate suppliers were our initial consulting partner and Air Academy Associates.

As with the management training assessment, we hand picked the participants in both face-off classes. We wanted objective, well respected participants to evaluate both classes. Similar to the management training assessments we had a portion of the class participants attend both training sessions and others who attended only one. We asked participants to comment on the workshops' overall effectiveness as well as the effectiveness of the instructor, printed materials and exercises. We were also interested on how the participants felt the materials were relevant to their jobs, the appropriateness of the depth and breadth of material covered and how much they personally valued the training session. As in the last analysis, all this individual class feedback data was collected for both sessions and analyzed for the sub-team charged with making a partner recommendation. This team's participants were also carefully selected to ensure all groups and perspectives were involved in the recommendation. With the exception of a couple individuals and myself (who facilitated the decision making process), the team members reviewing and recommending the Green Belt training partner were different from the team that made the management training recommendation. The overall process used was essentially the same as the one we used for the management training selection. We used a Delphi-like process with email questions to participants to solicit their individual responses and then a face-to-face meeting to review the initial outcome, debate the finer points and make the decision via a weighted Pugh matrix. As we saw in the management training decision, this process minimized the emotional issues and enabled a timely decision. After deliberation, the team recommended the Air Academy Associates Green Belt program, which was validated by the full DfLSS Launch Team.

With the decision to partner with the Air Academy, this completed the overall Lean Six Sigma roadmap (see Figure 3.6).[iv] The right half of this roadmap is the DMAIC/DMEDI roadmap illustrated earlier in Figure 2.1. The left side of this roadmap is intended for the product design portion of Xerox's Lean Six Sigma deployment. After determining that

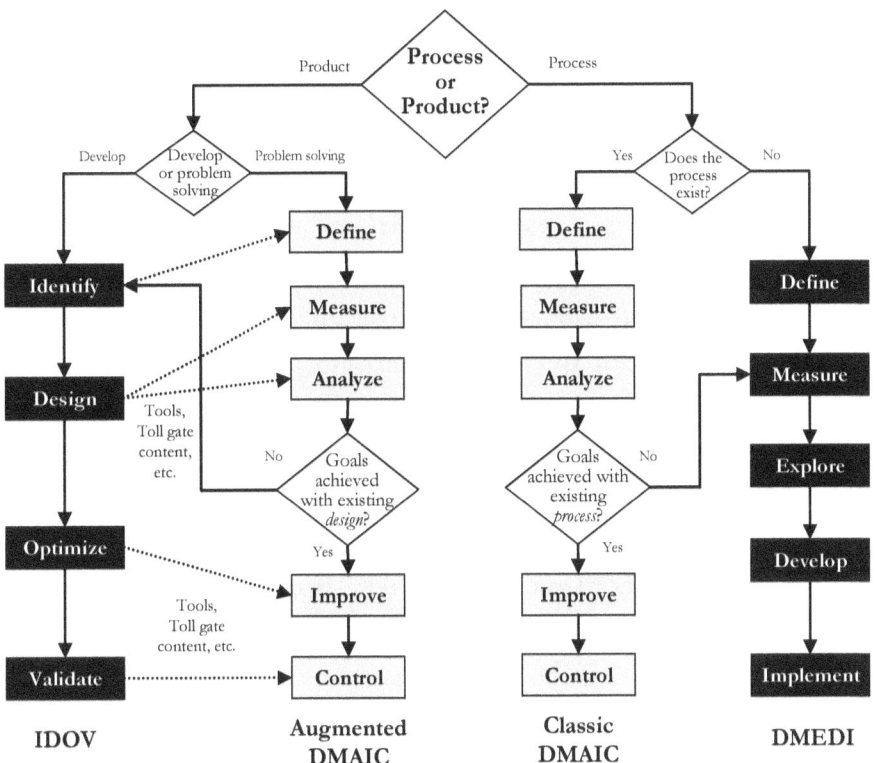

Figure 3.6: Xerox Lean Six Sigma Roadmap

you are dealing with a product, be it a full system, a subsystem or component, the next question was whether you are dealing with developing a product or solving a problem. If you are solving a problem, the DMAIC format worked well independent of whether it's a product or process related issue. For the product side of the map, we knew the DMAIC framework would work, but we had to augment the overall process with several of the DfLSS oriented tools and methods such as Design of Experiments, tolerance analysis and Robust Design. The decision was made to integrate the existing Air Academy Associates' IDOV process (or Identify, Design, Optimize and Validate) for the product development side of the Xerox Lean Six Sigma roadmap.

Developing, Integrating and Finalizing the DfLSS Training Content

With the new strategic training and coaching partner in hand, the next step was to blend the Air Academy Associates DfLSS content with our high level training view and certification requirements into an integrated package. The first item we looked at was including some level of DMAIC training to the DfLSS content. When we stepped back and looked at the product delivery based organizations' participation in the Lean Six Sigma DMAIC training initiatives, we saw that their involvement was not as extensive as one might have expected. One would have thought that the DMAIC process discipline and the extensive, statistics-based tools and methods would align well with the product delivery teams, but the data showed otherwise. The DfLSS Troika and the DfLSS Launch Team felt strongly that we needed to ensure all DfLSS participants had a good grounding in DMAIC tools for several reasons. Given the initial pressures to keep the Green Belt training to two weeks of class time, we knew that it was unrealistic to get the belt candidates exposed to all of the key Lean Six Sigma tools and methods. Second, our hypothesis was that Xerox's design-related processes (like any other work processes) were filled with wasteful steps which the DMAIC Lean Six Sigma training was intended to root out and eliminate. This hypothesis was later proven to be valid when we gave Design for Lean Six Sigma Green Belt candidates a homework assignment.

Between the two weeks of DfLSS Green Belt training we asked had hundreds of DfLSS Green Belts candidates take a normal work day in

58

their product delivery week, break it up into 15 minute blocks and then characterized if those blocks were Customer Value Added (CVA), Business Value Added (BVA) or Non-Value Added (NVA). Here we use Customer Value Added as those activities that are essential for delivering a product or service that the customer values and would pay for. Business Value Added can also be considered "necessary waste" in that they are activities that are deemed necessary for delivering a product or service, but that customers would typically be unwilling to pay for. A good example would be those business and financial activities necessary to meet Sarbanes-Oxley, Environmental Health and Safety or other critical government regulations. Finally, Non-Value Added can be defined as those activities that add no customer value and customers, if given the option, would not pay for them. In general, our DMAIC training was aimed at minimizing the Business Value Added work processes and eliminating the Non-Value Added work processes in order to maximize those Customer Value Added steps.

Data from Green Belt candidates can be found in Figure 3.7. The data indicated that only 30 percent of a product delivery professionals' time was Customer Value Added.[v] The remaining non-value added time was divided between Business Value Added time (38 percent) and Non-Value Added time (32 percent). Similar industry studies indicated these results were not unique to Xerox.[vi] This validated there was a huge opportunity in improving overall product delivery productivity by applying DMAIC methods and tools to our engineering work

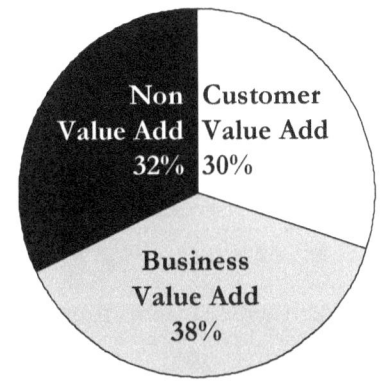

Figure 3.7: Xerox Engineering Value Add Analysis

processes. Even though DfLSS training and coaching was intended to optimize the Customer Value Added portion of an engineer's work, that data suggested there was an equally significant opportunity in eliminating the Non-Value Added and minimizing the Business Value Added portions of their daily activities. Even though every engineer may not personally conduct a DMAIC project aimed at Business or Non-Value Added reduction, they may participate in these projects and therefore they needed to understand the overall concepts. Therefore, we decided DfLSS belt candidates needed some fundamental DMAIC and Lean Six Sigma training.

To embed the DMAIC training into the overall DfLSS program, we decided to take a lesson from Xerox's DMAIC Green Belt program and add the MoreSteam.com Service Green Belt program into the DfLSS Green Belt curriculum. Given we wanted this background early in their educational experience we made the on-line portion of this curriculum a pre-requisite to the in-class DfLSS training. As in our DMAIC deployment, belt candidates were required to pass the set of embedded quizzes to get credit for the class and move on to the classroom training.

Keys to Success

Applying the DMAIC process to those Non-Value Added activities and distractions that prevent the product delivery community from spending a significant portion of their time doing what they have been paid to do will typically have a significant impact on overall effectiveness and efficiency.

One comment we heard from people taking the DMAIC on-line training is that the lessons often come across as a collection of individual Lean Six Sigma tools, not an integrated DMAIC process. We did not want the DfLSS belt candidates to walk away with that same impression. So, we added a one day DMAIC overview where we reviewed the DMAIC process, reminded them of the tools they learned on-line, introduced them to a few other Lean concepts and placed them into a simulation where they could apply the tools. We leveraged a majority the one day Lean Six Sigma training content previously taught to Finance personnel. At a high level, the simulation is a transactional process intentionally set up initially to be inefficient and ineffective. Through analysis of the collected data, process mapping and applying the tools taught in both the on-line training and in the one day DMAIC overview, teams would diagnosis the problems, eliminate the wasteful steps and approach six sigma-level performance. We felt it was important for Design for Lean Six Sigma belt candidates to "see" and "feel" the positive impacts of the DMAIC process.

Next we had to integrate the Air Academy Associates standard DfLSS training into the Xerox curriculum and certification structure. We realized that for a majority of the belt candidates just attending the training classes alone was not going to get them to the desired practioner competency level. So, the goal for the training was to get the Green Belt candidates to level 2 (individuals could perform some fundamental operations, but required guidance and support for a majority of the DfLSS methods and processes) and rely on execution of studies and coaching to get people to the desired competency level. At first, I had the impression that Air Academy leadership thought we were not on the right path with our DfLSS structure, but they followed along with our lead. The Air Academy Associates contracted Philip Mayfield as our Account Manager. His technical depth, teaching and coaching experience and his overwhelming enthusiasm helped as we attempted to integrate the content into a single curriculum. The standard Air Academy DfLSS Green Belt training included a combination of a Fundamentals week and a Capstone week. The Fundamentals week included many of the basic foundation tools that all participants needed to know. This included an introduction to probability, Measurement Systems Analysis and a significant amount of Design of Experiments (DoE) content. It also included exercising the suite of statistics and DoE software. The Air Academy utilizes software from SigmaZone and included *SPC XL* for basic statistical tools, *DOE Pro XL* for DoE analysis and *DFSS XL* for Monte Carlo, linear tolerancing and other DfLSS related tools.[vii] In reviewing these tools, we felt they would meet our initial needs. They had a very user friendly and intuitive human interface, they were powerful enough to meet the majority of our needs and they were fairly simple to learn. Another aspect that made these tools a success was that they were Microsoft Excel® add-ins. This became important given the deliberate Xerox DfLSS deployment strategy. By having the software as Excel® add-ins, it meant that people who had not been to training and did not have the software could open output results from others (who had the software) on their own personal computers and view the outputs. This was another one of those unintended positive consequences of our decision to use Air Academy Associates. Even though the software package were a perfect fit for our situation, the deployment team believed that a measure of our Design for Lean Six Sigma long term deployment success would be that our certified belts would grow to need a more sophisticated set of analytical software tools.

The standard Air Academy Fundamentals class was 4½ days. We needed to shave two hours on day one for the Xerox DfLSS burning platform and half day off the content to make room for the one day DMAIC overview and simulation day. This was accomplished through some minor compression of content. Though the instructors were not initially comfortable with the rather quick pace necessary to get through their materials in just four days, the Xerox belt candidates were able to keep up and enjoyed the rather intense four days. As a result, week one of the Xerox DfLSS Green Belt program included a pre-requisite of the MoreSteam.com on-line DMAIC Green Belt program, four days of Air Academy's Fundamentals (which included the one to two hour Xerox DfLSS burning platform), and a one day Xerox Master Black Belt taught DMAIC simulation day. This content remained fairly stable over the first three years of Xerox's DfLSS deployment, with the exception of the DfLSS burning platform. That changed approximately every quarter as we updated the platform presentation with quarterly Xerox financial performance, changes in the NVA/BVA/CVA engineering analysis and additions due to feedback from previous classes. The only other Fundamentals class change was a minor modification to the Measurement System Analysis module several months into the deployment when we found through our closed loop coaching feedback that belt candidates were not consistently picking up on the major points.

Week two of the DfLSS Green Belt training relied heavily on the standard Air Academy Capstone content.[viii] The only additions we made were adding about an hour worth of content on reliability (reliability overview, Accelerated Life Testing, Highly Accelerated Life Testing, etc.) and reference material on Xerox's Critical Parameter Management and high level modeling. All together, the DfLSS Green Belt training commitment for product delivery professionals was roughly 12-13 days, assuming 2-3 days for the on-line DMAIC training content.

The Electromechanical DfLSS Black Belt curriculum was our next challenge. We attempted to keep a couple of principles in play here. First, as indicated before, we wanted the Black Belt curriculum to build on top of the Green Belt curriculum. This was important as it ensured everyone had the same background going into the Black Belt classes, they all had mastered the Air Academy/SigmaZone software tools and that the Black Belt content would be incremental to what they learned during their Green Belt training. Second, we were conscious of the fact that the DfLSS Black Belt training commitment needed to be approximately the same as the DMAIC Black Belt training. As mentioned before, this was to ensure that both were perceived as being roughly "equal" minimizing the non-value added debate on which belt was more important. That meant that we were looking for approximately three incremental weeks of training content for Design for Lean Six Sigma Black Belts.

The Electromechanical Core Team then debated on where to "draw the line" on the DfLSS certification matrix of skills versus competency levels. In the DMAIC Black Belt model, the candidates were taken from their current job functions so they would be dedicated resources for tackling critical business problems in their respective Divisions. For DfLSS, Black Belts would be "in-position" or would remain in their current product delivery positions and use the DfLSS tools, methods and techniques to lead product delivery initiatives. As project and/or program leaders there were a set of skills that the Electromechanical Core Team felt were critical for Black Belt and Leaders to have above and beyond the standard Green Belt competencies.

One of the first Black Belt competencies that we tackled was project management. When reviewing both DMAIC and DfLSS Black Belt certified graduates we were surprised by their less than expected knowledge and use of basic project management tools and techniques. As this skill was essential for DfLSS (as well as DMAIC) Black Belts, we added a minimum of a level 3 (or practitioner) competency rating. Next, given the importance of partitioning and decomposing system level designs and flow down of system-level requirements and flow up of component, subsystem and system capability, we added incremental competency levels to both the System Design and Requirements Engineering best practice areas. We also felt it was necessary for Black Belts to demonstrate a higher proficiency in basic statistics, so we added one more level of competency (to a level 3) for the Statistical Tool Box best practice area. Knowing that Black Belts would be coaching Green Belt candidates in their mandatory level 3 in Design of Experiments, we added level 4 requirements for both Design of Experiments and Robust Design and Optimization Methods best practices. This was needed to fulfill the basic principle that a certifying coach must be at least one level of competency higher than the level they can certify to. Given we expected DfLSS Black Belts to eventually help coach their direct reports and potentially other Green Belts, we added a level 4 competency in the Coaching Best Practice area.

In the DfLSS Green Belt certification requirements, you may remember we gave each candidate the option of selecting two other best practice areas to get a level 3 mastery level. This enabled the Green Belt candidate to select those areas consistent with their current job function or where they were in their product delivery cycle. For Black Belts, we wanted to give a similar type of flexibility, so we added the certification

Keys to Success
Build enough Design for Lean Six Sigma certification flexibility in to support the various job functions and product delivery timing.

requirement that candidates needed at least two additional levels of mastery above the stated Black Belt certification minimum. That meant they could go from a level 2 to a level 4 in one best practice or jump from a level 2 to level 3 in two best practice areas.

With this basic certification structure in place, we began to fill in the training elements to meet those certification requirements. Because we felt that maximizing team performance was probably more important for a design team (given the relatively long time they are together versus a DMAIC project team), we wanted DfLSS Black Belts to go through a modified three day version of 3Circle Partners®' Team Accelerator which uses the Belbin profiles mentioned earlier in the book. The only modifications we made in the training was adding an introduction to Crucial Conversations® and using reduced cycles of learning to meet overall in class timing issues.

Xerox had a very good understanding and an internally developed tool set for breaking down systems and tracking the critical parameter flow down and capability flow up. So, we leveraged that expertise and created a two day training session that would give the Black Belt candidates the skills necessary to meet the System Design and Requirements

Engineering requirements. This Critical Parameter Management (CPM) and modified Team Accelerator training content made up one full week of training.

As mentioned previously, for many effective coaching can be tougher to master than project and/or people management. To help DMAIC Black Belts with their coaching skills, a blended learning class was developed. It included an on-line training prerequisite and a one day instructor-led session that included material review and various role play exercises. Since we knew coaching would also be a challenge for Design for Lean Six Sigma Black Belts, we decided to make it a mandatory class and a certification requirement for all DfLSS Black Belt candidates.

Next, we engaged SigmaZone and Air Academy Associates to help develop what would be known as the Electromechanical Black Belt Common Week. The course outline was developed by taking the defined Black Belt best practice minimum best practice area competency levels and asking Air Academy what they saw were the most common and complex areas Green Belts were getting themselves into when their Master Black Belts were coaching our belt candidates. Given the extensive Green Belt coaching the Air Academy Master Black Belts were involved with, this information was readily available. Together, we went through the various best practice requirements and complex Green Belt questions and selected a series of advanced Black Belt topics. These included Advanced DoE topics and Comparison of Robust Design Techniques, Regression Statistics, and Optimization using Deterministic Modeling. The good news was that some of these topics had already been developed and training materials were available. For those items it became just a packaging issue to put it into a usable format and structure. The other topics had to be developed and integrated by Air Academy Associates and SigmaZone with the already available content. Overall, this process went very well and we ended up with a five day Common Black Belt Week of training that received high praise from the Black Belt candidates' feedback.

The last week of Black Belt training was named Electromechanical Black Belt Flexible Week. This week of training was intended to support the Black Belt candidates' requirement for the two levels of best practice mastery beyond the minimum standard requirements. To enable this, we had two basic paths: either taking a "standard" DfLSS elective or allowing Black Belt candidates to choose other external training options. Standard DfLSS electives were targeted at higher proficiency on one specific best practice area or where we could leverage the existing training classes within the Lean Six Sigma or Xerox Corporate offerings. For example, we partnered with ReliaSoft® to develop a class to meet a minimum of a level 3 Reliability Methods best practice area. The documented level 3 requirements were consistent with their existing reliability training content. The only thing necessary was to add two ReliaSoft® coaching sessions to establish their study charter that would meet those best practice requirements and inspect the work done by the Black Belt candidate. We also were leveraging internal Xerox Subject Matter Experts to deliver advanced classes on topics such as Advanced Modeling and Simulation. Since existing DMAIC Black and Green Belt training fit within several DfLSS best practice areas (such as Statistical Tool Box and Lean Development), the decision was made to allow DfLSS credit for this type of training. For coach validation of these best practices, we utilized the existing Xerox DMAIC Master Black Belt population. The external training option was intended to give a high degree of flexibility to the Black Belt candidate.

We realized that it would be almost impossible to develop an extensive list of high level classes to fit the wide range of product delivery professionals' needs. So, we gave Black Belt candidates an option to go to college courses, external training seminars and other means to get the incremental knowledge and skills necessary for their certifications. The only requirements we put on them was (1) any external training had to be pre-approved by their DfLSS Deployment Manager and the Corporate Lean Six Sigma Office prior to taking the class, (2) that it had to be "recent" or within the last year or so, (3) that it had to tie directly to one of the DfLSS Best Practice areas and (4) we needed to have the course instructor's signature and acknowledgement of the project evidence that you met the best practice competency requirements. Given this path was a bit more involved, most of the initial waves of Black Belt candidates chose one of the standard Black Belt options. Figure 3.8 illustrates the Design for Lean Six Sigma Green Belt and Black Belt training content.

		Time To **Complete**
Black Belt	Black Belt Flexible Week	5 days
	Black Belt Common Week	5 days
	Coaching for Success	1+ day
	Critical Parameter Management (CPM) / Team Accelerator	5 days
Green Belt	Capstone Workshop	5 days
	Fundamentals Workshop / DMAIC Lean Day	5 days
	On-Line DMAIC/Statistical Tools	2-3 days

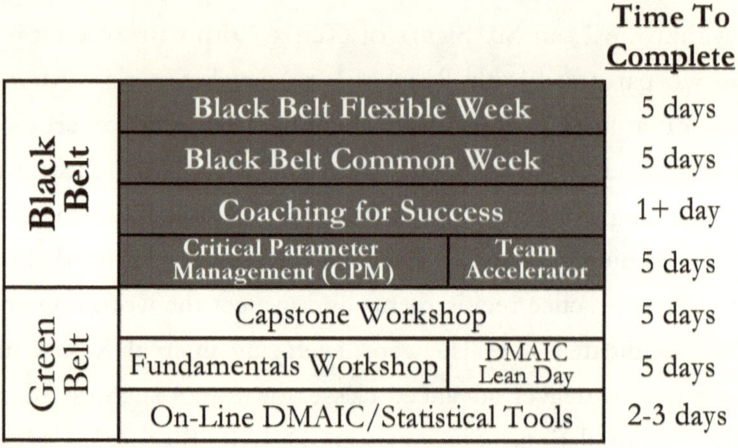

**Figure 3.8: Design for Lean Six Sigma
Green Belt and Black Belt Training Content**

Just as we did in the DfLSS Green Belt program, we utilized the Air Academy Associate's Master Black Belt coaches to review Black Belt candidates' competency levels and sign off for their certification. Because the incremental standard Black Belt skill levels were all at or above Level 3, each required studies to meet the certification requirement. Since these studies tended to be more complex to meet the more demanding skill definitions we gave each Black Belt candidate access to eight incremental coaching sessions. We also spaced the Black Belt coaching sessions to six weeks between sessions to allow more time to complete these more complex studies.

Quickly, our Black Belt curriculum was put to the test as Black Belt candidates created a set of challenges for the Division Deployment Managers. In general, demand to get into the Black Belt program exceeded the supply of available seats given the fixed DfLSS budget. This made the Deployment Managers look closely at their respective Division's needs analyzing how best to trade off other DfLSS training "seats" for Black Belts and selecting the best Black Belt candidates for their allocated seats. The word "best" has many different meanings here. Not only were we focused on the most highly skilled individuals, but also those in the best situation. By that I mean that candidates had managers who believed in Design for Lean Six Sigma and would create a supportive environment for the Black Belt candidates (or any belt for that matter) to effectively practice their newly acquired skills. This supportive

Keys to Success

Having a supportive work environment where the belt candidate can practice these newly found DfLSS skills should be a critical criteria for selecting belt candidates for training.

environment could include other Black Belt candidates, DfLSS-oriented Subject Matter Experts, DfLSS Green Belts, etc. Without this supportive environment, it would be easy to fall prey to "old group norms" and fall back to the way designs were developed prior to DfLSS. We were fortunate that the DfLSS Deployment Managers understood the critical nature and importance of the Black Belt selection process. The first several waves of Black Belt candidates were great advocate representatives for the DfLSS program. They were technical leaders within their respective organizations, had supportive environments and their work and accompanying results were highly visible to not only middle to upper management, but to their direct reports and peers. This created even more "pull" from people to enter not only the Black Belt program, but also gave credibility to the entire Design for Lean Six Sigma program as well.

Finalizing Certification Requirements, Quizzes and Remediation

As we completed the high level curriculum and content details, we had to document the Design for Lean Six Sigma Green and Black Belt certification requirements. The list below highlights the Green Belt certification specifics:

- Successfully complete a minimum of the on-line Service DMAIC Green Belt training by scoring a cumulative 80 percent or better correct on the quizzes.

- Successfully complete the DfLSS Fundamentals class by scoring an 80 percent or better correct on the quiz.

- Successfully complete the DfLSS Capstone class by scoring a cumulative 80 percent or better correct on the quiz.

- Successfully demonstrate mastery of the designated Green Belt DfLSS best practice competencies and skills to your assigned coach. This will include a minimum of three Level 3 or higher current best practice studies and teachbacks for the remaining best practice areas. A current study is one that is initiated specifically to be associated with the training.

- Demonstrate to and receive endorsement from the Green Belt Candidate's Manager or Project Sponsor for mastery of (a) ability to produce results that are valued by the Unit, (b) team leadership and (c) coaching ability.

As stated before, the Design for Lean Six Sigma Black Belt certification required that candidates successfully complete their DfLSS Green Belt certification before entering into the Black Belt curriculum. The Black Belt certification requirements therefore would include the Design for Lean Six Sigma Green Belt requirements above, plus the following:

- Successfully complete the DfLSS Team Accelerator class.

- Successfully complete the Critical Parameter Management class by scoring an 80 percent or better correct on the quiz.

- Successfully complete the on-line and instructor-led portions of the Coaching for Success class.

- Successfully complete the DfLSS Black Belt Common Week class by scoring an 80 percent or better on the quiz.

- Successfully complete either a standard DfLSS Black Belt Flexible Week class or an approved external class with at least an equivalent of 35 hours of training that aligns to one of the best practice areas. Completion is characterized by scoring an 80 percent or better on the assigned quiz(zes).

- Successfully demonstrate mastery of the designated Black Belt DfLSS best practice competencies and skills to your assigned coach. This will include a minimum of seven Level 3 or higher current best practice studies and teachbacks for the remaining best practice areas.

- Demonstrate to and receive endorsement of the Black Belt Candidate's Manager or Project Sponsor for mastery of (a) ability to produce results that are valued by the Unit, (b) team leadership and (c) coaching ability.

Once a belt candidate completed his or her certification requirements, they collected up their signed off study charters, validated best practice competencies and other critical supporting documents. These would be sent to their DfLSS Deployment Managers who would validate that the candidate met all the requirements, completed the work and had all of the proper signatures. Since the Deployment Managers owned the certification process, some would also add some additional requirements such as setting up face-to-face meetings with each belt candidate or having the candidate present their completed studies to a panel of Master

Black Belts. Once convinced that the candidate had met the belt requirements, the Deployment Manager would initiate a request for certification and forward the entire package to the Lean Six Sigma Corporate Office. There a team of Lean Six Sigma Corporate Office Master Black Belts would review the documents for consistency within and across the various Xerox Divisions. Once validated by the Master Black Belts the centralized database of Lean Six Sigma belt certifications

Keys to Success

Celebrate certifications in a public forum. It can communicate importance of the accomplishment and identify belts as who people can go to for program information, advice, etc.

would be updated and a plaque would be generated acknowledging the belt's certification accomplishments. Often these plaques would be presented to the certified individuals at communication meetings or other public sessions to maximize the exposure of their accomplishments to others.

The Design for Lean Six Sigma quizzes were developed in conjunction with the Air Academy. The quizzes consisted of twenty-five multiple choice questions covering the range of material presented during each week of training. To be consistent with the DMAIC training, all the quizzes were open book and open notes. Our intention was not to make the quizzes exceedingly difficult. We knew that with our coaching model, there were several learning cycles available to insure that belt candidates knew and mastered the desired skills. We intentionally made a few questions relatively easy, a few which could be characterized as being relatively tricky and more difficult and the balance of medium difficulty. One of the quiz questions in particular typically would trip up almost half the belt candidates. It was not that the question was excessively difficult. In fact, when we gave the belt candidates who got it wrong the right answer, they shook their heads and realized the simple mistake they made. Thinking that maybe we did not reinforce the key learning point enough, we repeated it several times during the next series of training weeks and again in the reviews before the quiz. The extra reinforcement did not seem to make any difference as roughly the same percentage of belt candidates kept missing the same question. There was some pressure to change the question, but we kept it in the quiz as it typically did not put belt candidates at risk of not passing the quiz. It also had the positive impact that when those who missed the question were told the answer, they never forgot the learning point again.

One common question we heard often was "why are quizzes required for certification?" This was done for several reasons. First, we wanted to collect data on both within a class and across classes over time how well the skills and knowledge were being transferred to the belt candidates. One could argue that a quiz score is not the best measure of how well knowledge has actually been transferred. In reality, that probably is true. The ability to apply the procedural knowledge is probably an overall better measure of the knowledge transfer effectiveness. But we did not want to wait until the training and coaching were completed to find out that a critical topic or concept was not completely understood. Therefore, one may look at the resulting quiz scores as in-process measures of knowledge transfer. The second reason was that we wanted to create another cycle of learning. A quiz let belt candidates know what concepts they mastered and ones that they did not. That enabled the belt candidate a baseline from which they can plan out what incremental work, if necessary, was needed to get them to the desired level of competency. Knowing what they did not understand, allows belt candidates insight to where they may also need to challenge some of their basic and underlying assumptions. Third, as mentioned above, the quiz allowed the opportunity to catch those critical concepts that a belt candidate may have missed. By remediating them as soon as possible, we help ensure that the students adequately understand the various key topics and were not left behind. Finally, and maybe most importantly, having a quiz at the end of class helped maintain a belt candidate's focus during the class. If belt candidate knows they are going to be quizzed on what was taught they are more likely to pay attention, limit their external distractions and stay engaged with the class and instructor.

Even with all the positives associated with giving quizzes, we were conscious of the fact that putting too much emphasis on the quizzes can be damaging as well. After going through hundreds of DMAIC and Design for Lean Six Sigma class and quiz cycles, we found we had to take steps to lower the quiz anxiety level of many belt candidates. We initially would just tell students on the first day of training that they would be quizzed the last day of that week's training. As the week went on, we found many belt candidates starting to become overly anxious about the quiz. The more they worried, the more they became overly distracted from the presented content. That anxiety often culminated with students studying all night even though they were told before the quiz that it would be multiple choice questions and open book. I personally observed several people actually having what appeared to be a severe anxiety

Keys to Success

Though quizzes are important, the successful application of the methods and tools in the work environment that is the true test if the belt candidate has mastered the skills.

attacks while taking the quiz. That was never the desired outcome that we were looking for. After observing this behavior in several classes, we began to tell students up front that there would be a quiz and emphasizing that it would be open book, open note but not open partner (trying to add a bit of levity and reduce the tension). We also took steps to lower that anxiety level by letting them know that a significant majority of the belt candidates pass the test and if they paid attention in class that they would likely pass as well.

We also incorporated several different content review methods to help give belt candidates more cycles of learning and show them the type of questions that may be asked on the quizzes. One technique that we used in the DMAIC classes was to incorporate teachbacks in the classes. Here, teams were set up, assigned various topics that were taught that week and were asked to teach it back to the rest of the class. Armed with only flip charts and pens, each belt candidate had a fixed time to review the key points of their assigned topic. The teachbacks were conducted just prior to the quiz and the flip charts were left hanging on the walls so they could be referenced by the class during the exam. If a belt candidate missed a critical point during their teachback, the Master Black Belt instructor would step in and remind the class of the points that were missed. This proved to be a very powerful method of reinforcing the important points of the training and giving students another cycle of learning.

Even with all of the efforts to reduce the stress, we could not totally eliminate the high level of quiz anxiety in some of the belt candidates. As a result, instructors became more vigilant to the anxiety warning signs and helped those individuals that exhibited trouble handling the stress of the quiz. One such technique we found effective was allowing belt candidates exhibiting excessive levels of anxiety to take the test in private. This turned out to help many candidates because they were not negatively influenced by those who completed the quiz early. I observed that as more people in any given class completed the quiz (passing it or not), those remaining felt increasing pressure to finish. This negatively added stress to those left and increased their level of anxiety. Since the quiz was open book, taking it in private did not impact the integrity of the quiz or its results. It also insured that the test environment was quiet. As people completed their quiz and collected their belongings, it created noise which some found distracting.

Another common question asked by some belt candidates is "what if I do not pass one of the quizzes?" Quiz remediation was achieved through multiple ways. The first option was for the class instructor to sit with the belt candidate who did not pass the quiz immediately after they have taken the quiz to assess their knowledge on the topics that they missed. After giving quizzes to thousands of DMAIC and DfLSS belt candidates, we realized that people may have a satisfactory working knowledge of the quiz topics, but as a result of other factors, the candidate may not necessarily score well on the quiz. For adult learners who are far along in their careers and have been out of college or other educational institutions for an extended period of time, it may have been decades since they had to take a quiz or been tested. Throw in issues associated with various learning disabilities, English as a second language and other barriers; it is not surprising the high level of anxiety that can exist when some adults take tests. We empowered the class room instructors with the ability to grant a passing grade of 80 percent to those who scored less than that standard if the belt candidate could demonstrate to the instructor's satisfaction they had an acceptable working knowledge of the topics they missed. This was the most popular option as it dealt with the missed questions immediately and it ensured the students understood the critical topics before they entered their next class or started coaching.

If the belt candidate could not be remediated at the end of the class, we would set up coaching sessions to make sure they understood the content. Our concern was that the Green Belt Capstone week built on the foundation of the first week of Green Belt Fundamentals content. If belt candidates had issues with the Fundamental content, they would typically fall further behind in the Capstone class. The last opportunity to remediate those who did not pass one of the quizzes was during the scheduled post-class coaching sessions. Here, we would have their assigned coach validate that the belt candidate has mastered the areas they did not get correct during their quizzes. For each method, signatures from the instructor or coach and their DfLSS Deployment Manager were required before the candidate could be certified.

Generating Contagious Design for Lean Six Sigma Commitment

As much as all those actively involved in developing and delivering the Xerox Design for Lean Six Sigma program thought it was the right thing to do, we knew we had to also deal with the cultural acceptance by managers, engineers and everyone else involved in product delivery. Without winning the "hearts and minds" of our research, design and delivery community we could fall victim to the power of maintaining the status quo.   After doing some research in this area, we converged on inviting Dr. Andrea Shapiro for a one day session focused on her book *Creating Contagious Commitment*.[ix] Though there were several key points in her book and presentation, the one item that the DfLSS Troika and the rest of the Design for Lean Six Sigma deployment team members picked up on were the seven levers of change. These levers of changes are as follows:

1. Contacts between advocates and apathetics
2. Mass exposure
3. Hiring advocates
4. Removing resisters
5. Walk the talk
6. Ensuring reward and recognition supports the change
7. Making sure that the infrastructure is in place to support the change

The goal is to utilize the interdependency of these seven levers to influence individual's commitment to change and drive toward the Tipping Point where the change initiative is embraced by an organization. Let's take each of these one at a time and discuss what actions were taken to support the levers of change.

The first lever is encouraging contacts between advocates and apathetics. Andrea used the term advocate to identify those people who are enthusiastic about the cultural change and apathetics as those who are disconnected from the cultural change or are not affected by it. It is the contact between advocates and apathetics that can build enthusiasm and build change momentum. As the Electromechanical Core Team and Deployment Managers assessed people within the Xerox product delivery organizations, there was an effort to identify the existing pockets of excellence that were currently utilizing the Design for Lean Six Sigma methods and tools. These individuals served not only as a great source for Xerox examples needed to integrate into the training, but also a pool of people who would be excellent candidates to go through the

Keys to Success

Make sure you allocate time, effort and resources to address the cultural transformation needed to ensure a pervasive and sustainable deployment.

Green Belt training. One advantage of training these people first is that they were typically very familiar with the methods and tools and were able to immediately apply them their assigned delivery objectives. This helped to build the library of good Xerox Design for Lean Six Sigma examples. The apathetic product design professionals often needed real Xerox examples to help increase the probability of moving them to incubators (or those willing to consider the cultural change and how it impacts them and their work) and ultimately advocates. Several Divisions took the opportunity to set up "lunch and learn" sessions that gave these advocates the opportunity to share their DfLSS successes with their peers and others. These started slow, but gained momentum as the number of Xerox examples and the number of Design for Lean Six Sigma belts being trained grew. It was also a way for those not selected for near term training to find out more what DfLSS was all about. These became a very popular forum for advocates to discuss Design for Lean Six Sigma related topics not only with apathetics, but also other advocates.

One other opportunity that we jumped on during our first year of deployment was to participate in an internal modeling and simulation conference. We were able to convince conference organizers to give us several sessions for Design for Lean Six Sigma presentations. We engaged the Air Academy coaches to help identify the best studies and use of Design for Lean Six Sigma tools they had seen. With five or six months of deployment behind us, there were more than enough great examples to choose from. Because this conference was open to the entire product delivery community, we had numerous apathetics and incubators in the audience who were at least mildly interested on what was going on. The high quality papers and presentations from various product design groups gave advocates opportunities to engage those sitting on the acceptance fence. The planned breakout sessions also gave advocates and apathetics the opportunity to sit down and discuss Design for Lean Six Sigma. In the following years, the presence of Design for Lean Six Sigma in this conference increased. This included more sessions dedicated to DfLSS and invited keynote speaker slots assigned to the DfLSS program. All together, we found the conference gave people a number of opportunities to create contacts between advocates and apathetics.

Our Design for Lean Six Sigma program development and deployment did not allow us to gear up mass exposure efforts as early as we wanted. Though several things were done to take advantage of the mass exposure lever, we were careful to overemphasize mass exposure and balance it with the other levers of change. One action we took was placing several Design for Lean Six Sigma related articles on the internal Xerox intranet site. We started by selected several very good studies and projects to highlight as well as role model managers that supported the overall Design for Lean Six Sigma initiative. These articles highlighted various successes we had solving problems that had lingered for extended periods of time, new designs that were delivered more efficiently, effectively and predictably and what managers could do to support and encourage Design for Lean Six Sigma methods and tools usage. These would be inserted into the Xerox intranet site and remain there for several days at a time. This became a very popular forum to expose the product design community and those not intimately involved in product delivery what Design for Lean Six Sigma was all about.

There also were several video taped testimonials from practicing Design for Lean Six Sigma belts discussing their successes associated with applying the methods and tools. These were shown as various communications meetings and distributed to key deployment people so they could be shared with others. One could also count the Design for Lean Six Sigma papers given at the internal Xerox modeling and simulation conference mentioned above as another venue for mass exposure.

Within each Division, the Deployment Managers played an important role in helping not only support the development and deployment of Design for Lean Six Sigma, but also disseminate information within the respective units. They encouraged key leaders to incorporate Design for Lean Six Sigma and how important it was for the long term success of their Division in their various management communications. We also gave the Deployment Managers electronic copies of the Design for Lean Six Sigma Burning Platform presentations to use for those not initially selected to take the training. This helped communicate what the training was, why Xerox was embarking on this significant task and the importance of their roles in delivering effective and efficient technologies and designs.

All of these mass communication methods supported the overall success of the deployment, but looking back we could have done more, earlier to drive the message home. One barrier we faced was that the pressure to start the overall deployment was high, driving us to start the training before we had finished developing all the critical training, certification and infrastructure details and collaterals. At times it felt like we were laying down the railroad tracks as the Design for Lean Six Sigma train was rolling down the track. During the training and coaching, belt candidates would ask important and reasonable questions on topics like certification requirements and Black Belt training specifics. Unfortunately, on several occasions we either did not have the answer because we had not taken the time to work on that topic or the potential solution had not been agreed to by the Divisions or Design for Lean Six Sigma Launch Team. For what ever reason, it caused some frustration on the belts' parts as we did not have all the answers up front. In hind sight, it probably would have been more advantageous to strike a better balance between finalizing all the program and deployment details and communicate the total package to the masses upfront versus deploying faster and developing some of the program specifics as we went along.

Given the business state of Xerox at the time, we did not have many opportunities to hire Design for Lean Six Sigma advocates. There was limited overall product design related hiring and those who were hired tended to be part of Xerox's college recruitment program. Though some new college hires were familiar with the Design for Lean Six Sigma methods and tools, they most likely would not have an immediate impact influencing their new work environments as compared with someone with significant experience and results would have. The hiring of advocates became less of a priority as our deployment moved forward. We were fortunate that a robust candidate selection process and an outstanding pool of Design for Lean Six Sigma candidates yielded not only technically skilled belts, but individuals who had the interactive skills to be effective advocates. As the number of training classes and coaching sessions increased, we realized we had a better chance at developing successful Design for Lean Six Sigma program advocates from within Xerox than acquiring them through external hires.

In her workshop, Andrea indicated that removing resisters is one of the three levers that should be used very carefully (the other two being mass communication and hiring advocates). Overall, we had little necessity to take action on removing resisters. Early in our deployment, we wanted to hear the resisters' comments and concerns. As our deployment continued, we were able to let the impressive results of the Design for Lean Six Sigma studies and projects speak for themselves. Also, because not all people had the opportunity for training, it was difficult to go to design-related managers and have them remove resisters before they had the chance to at least participate in the entire program.

During the early stages of our deployment, we were actually interested in what apathetics and resisters had to say. In many cases, they helped identify certain shortfalls with the program that needed to be corrected. Their comments helped us identify issues, fix specific problems and strengthening the overall Design for Lean Six Sigma program. Though not formally removed, there was pressure indirectly applied to resisters as managers and others in their respective organizations began to adopt Design for Lean Six Sigma principles. As managers began asking teams to "show me the data" responses typically illustrated a gap between those who had been through the training and those who had not. As more people within an organization became trained and started using their new methods and tools, the past group norms were replaced with more efficient and effective Design for Lean Six Sigma practices. The more resisters relied on past design methods, the bigger the overall performance gap became. As the overall performance gap grew, so did the pressure to conform to the newly established Design for Lean Six Sigma group norms. Resisters were soon faced with either adopting the organization's new work environment or moving to another assignment. Looking forward, as Xerox approaches the goal of one hundred percent of the eligible product delivery professionals trained in at least Design for Lean Six Sigma Green Belt I believe there will be fewer places for resisters to hide, meaning resisters must either adopt Design for Lean Six Sigma or make a career change decision.

From a "walk the talk" perspective, there were several items that supported this lever of change. Here we are focused on managers and key leaders "walking the talk" and supporting the Design for Lean Six Sigma initiative by living it on a regular basis. We were fortunate in that we have many managers who believed in the Design for Lean Six Sigma methodologies and were looking for a broader deployment of these tools within their units and across the product delivery community. As it was mentioned before, we started our Design for Lean Six Sigma deployment by training the product delivery managers first. During those training sessions, it was fairly clear which managers really understood and supported the initiative and those who did not. With the constrained deployment, Deployment Managers were faced with focusing on which group would be given the training priority. In most cases, it was not only those areas where there were historical high failure rates and total cost of ownership, but priorities were also given to those organizations who's leaders demonstrated their overall acceptance of the Design for Lean Six Sigma process. Our hypothesis was that if managers thought favorably of and supported Design for Lean Six Sigma, the higher the probably of successfully implementing it in their respective organizations. Therefore, those managers that were "walking the talk" were in many cases rewarded by getting training priority in the constrained environment.

We also were fortunate enough to have managers who felt it was necessary to demonstrate their commitment to the program by participating in the extensive Design for Lean Six Sigma training. We had middle to upper managers who completed both the on-line DMAIC training and sat through the two weeks of instructor-led Design for Lean Six Sigma Green Belt training. This not only gave them a deeper understanding of the methods and tools, but also communicated that the Design for Lean Six Sigma initiative was important to their respective organizations. Even with all of their business priorities, over committed calendars and other challenges, they found the time to sit through and actively participate in the training. One critical person that needs to be mentioned is Quincy Allen, President of Xerox's Production Systems Group. He took time out of his demanding calendar to sit through and fully participated in the two weeks of Design for Lean Six Sigma Green Belt training. To Quincy's credit, he sat through the entire two week sessions with basically no interruptions from outside the classroom. This sent an incredibly important message through not only his organization, but the other product development related organizations as well. He backed up his words of how important Design for Lean Six Sigma was to Xerox and the success of the Production Systems Group by personally carving out the time to fully participate in the classroom instruction. That is senior leadership walking the talk!

Another item that supported walk the talk lever was the Design for Lean Six Sigma burning platform. In that document, we illustrated the link between key Xerox business metrics to the current product delivery effectiveness, efficiency and predictability as well as how Design for Lean Six Sigma could be used to improve the overall product delivery performance. We also illustrated how Design for Lean Six Sigma aligned to Anne Mulcahy's and the Corporation's high level objectives. Making all of these linkages helped many see how Design for Lean Six Sigma fit within Xerox and its objectives. The Design for Lean Six Sigma burning platform also helped communicate the overall vision of the program. As mentioned, this was given at the start of every Green Belt training session. It was also discussed during the management training and was given to Deployment Managers so they could use the document for other internal communication sessions.

Changing established reward and recognition systems within any large corporation can be a challenge. In this case, we are asking managers and other leaders, many of who got their positions through product design techniques that we were trying to change, to reward people for using Design for Lean Six Sigma philosophies. Though some leaders got it immediately, we knew it would be much longer before rewarding the new Design for Lean Six Sigma behavior would be fully integrated. There were areas where we did make progress however. An example was having a Division President communicate that critical product design positions within their Division in the future would require a Design for Lean Six Sigma Black Belt certification. This helped set the expectation that if you wanted to be considered for those positions, you would need to become DfLSS Black Belt. This created even more pull by the design community for not only the Black Belt but also the first Design for Lean Six Sigma building block, Green Belt certification. To support this position, a higher proportion of that Division's Green and Black Belt training seats intentionally went to individuals currently in or those aspiring to those key product design management positions. This helped incumbent Design for Lean Six Sigma certified managers looking for their next promotion upward and solidified the Black Belt certification bar for those looking to be promoted into those critical leadership positions.

Overall, recognition was easier to administer than reward. Many Divisions gave out the Design for Lean Six Sigma certification plaques in public communications meetings to not only recognize those who had achieved their certification but also highlight their impressive contributions. It also showed the balance of the organization who they could go to if they had Design for Lean Six Sigma questions. We also highlighted several managers and Design for Lean Six Sigma belts in feature articles at Xerox's intranet site. Again, we wanted to give those leaders and major DfLSS contributors the appropriate recognition for their efforts. Video clip testimonials highlighting Design for Lean Six Sigma accomplishments and successes were made and distributed to Deployment Managers for their use during various communication functions. The previously mentioned Design for Lean Six Sigma papers given at the internal Xerox modeling and simulation conference could also be considered recognition as only the best examples from literally hundreds of submissions were selected and presented to their design peers.

The last lever is insuring the proper infrastructure is in place to support the cultural change. We were fortunate in that we could leverage some of the established DMAIC Lean Six Sigma infrastructure for Design for Lean Six Sigma initiative. This included those individuals and practices in place to support such things as training class registration, records retention, certification validation and others. It added a small burden on the existing infrastructure resources, but helped keep the overall Design for Lean Six Sigma infrastructure costs to a minimum. That enabled more financial resources that could be applied to Design for Lean Six Sigma training and coaching. Early on Deployment Managers were designated in each product delivery Division specifically for the Design for Lean Six Sigma initiative. This meant Divisions utilized full time dedicated resources to support development and deployment of DfLSS within their respective units. These Deployment Managers not only were our advocates registering belt candidates, supporting certification and pushing information through there organizations but they also acted as a conduit for product delivery personnel voice of the customer to those of us working out the training content and certification requirements. The Deployment Manager played an important role in the successful development and deployment of the Design for Lean Six Sigma initiative.

One infrastructure challenge we had was the Design for Lean Six Sigma funding and available training seat constraints. Though everyone involved in the Design for Lean Six Sigma fully supported the initiative, the budget constraints almost doubled the total time necessary to train and certify one hundred percent of the eligible product design community. Though other trade-offs, sacrifices and changes to the program contemplated aimed at increasing the Design for Lean Six Sigma funding level; it still was not enough to make a significant dent into the total time necessary to train everyone. Our hope was that we could establish the early momentum and sustain it over the several years needed to complete the training. Why was the time necessary to get fully trained significant? Even though we had hundreds of successfully completed studies and projects, until most (if not all) of the people working on those subsystems were Design for Lean Six Sigma trained, we were never going to see the full impact the initiative had to offer. Total product delivery effectiveness and efficiency would always be greatly influenced by the weakest link in the delivery chain. By that, those not following the Design for Lean Six Sigma methods and principles would typically have longer delivery times with less robust subsystems. Until Design for Lean Six Sigma became the way a significant majority of the delivery team worked, we most likely would not see significant breakthrough in the overall, high level program delivery metrics. Therefore, as Deployment Managers worked through their seat allocation priorities, more were looking at getting complete design teams trained, sometimes together, to ensure maximum overall delivery effectiveness.

Having Dr. Shapiro's seven levers of change constantly in front of us made sure the Design for Lean Six Sigma deployment community were conscious of how we could impact the overall pervasiveness and sustainability of the entire initiative.

Assessing Design for Lean Six Sigma Training and Program Results

With the curriculum set, partners selected and certification requirements established, we started the task of training the Xerox electromechanical product delivery professionals. We choose to take the DfLSS training to the various research and design centers around the globe versus having them come to a central training facility. This helped minimize the time we were taking away from their full time design positions by traveling. To assess how the belt candidates felt about the overall training experience, we developed and maintained a four page belt candidate evaluation and feedback survey. We asked questions about the overall effectiveness of the training as well as the effectiveness of the instructor, hands-on exercises and printed materials. Looking at the belt candidate feedback, it was clear that they liked the DfLSS training. Feedback included a numerical rating system and space allotted for belt candidate written comments. The number scores and written comments confirmed that the belt candidates were impressed with the training and its applicability to their jobs. Belt candidates were also very impressed with the Air Academy Associates' instructors. Written comments validated that the Air Academy instructors were able to effectively connect with and transfer knowledge to the students in the class room. Belt candidates also were impressed with the various printed materials they were given, the exercises that they participated in and the overall flow of the class.

Overall, the belt candidates were also pleased with the overall length and pace of the training. These two items were initially concerns for the overall deployment. There was a great deal of pressure to keep the training to roughly two weeks. Add in the on-line DMAIC training prerequisite and most people had invested almost three weeks for DfLSS Green Belt training time. We felt this was pushing the initial timing envelop we were given. As the feedback results came in we were happy to see that the training length was not a barrier. We were also concerned about the pace. As stated earlier, we needed to compress the typical four and a half day Fundamentals class to four to accommodate the DMAIC and Lean training day. We also added roughly one to three hours of incremental training content to the standard Air Academy Fundamentals and Capstone offerings. Even though the instructors initially felt a bit uncomfortable with the quicker training pace, the students felt that it was "just right". I believe the success of this accelerated training content is a testament to the skills of the Xerox's research, design and product development professionals and the class room management capability of the Air Academy Associates instructors.

Given the proprietary nature of the products that Xerox develops and delivers, it's difficult to get into specifics associated with projects and studies conducted with the DfLSS trained belts. In general, the belts and belt candidates who applied the DfLSS tools, methods and principles found their design solutions were more robust against noises, completed in a fraction of the time as compared with past designs with similar complexity and they felt confident that the designs or technologies would work right the first time. These DfLSS trained product development professionals became more efficient, effective and predictable in their delivery of technologies and designs. Right from the beginning of the DfLSS deployment, technical problems that had been lingering for years were solved in a matter of months. This helped gain important credibility with skeptical management and other product delivery personnel. Quincy Allen, President of Xerox's Production Systems Group and who was a trained DfLSS Green Belt, indicated that the previous design and development work process for a new product could take up to 18 months, however "using the DfLSS approach we did it in five months." [x] He went on to say that "the product worked exactly the way we thought it would work and at the level of defects we thought it would have." When asked about the translating that DfLSS product delivery success into impacting the Xerox bottom line financials, Mr. Allen indicated "I spend the same number of engineering dollars and get twice what I did before."

One Xerox Design for Lean Six Sigma example that is in the public domain is an article written by Bob Hildebrand.[xi] In this article, Bob documented the work done on a photoreceptor belt tensioning system modification on the Xerox iGen3® color printer. Bob, a certified DfLSS Black Belt, used the IDOV (Identify, Design, Optimize and Validate) framework to walk through how he and his team accomplished their complicated design challenge. Through the systematic use of a series of Taguchi, central composite design and nearly orthogonal Latin hypercube sampling Design of Experiments as well as blending both low fidelity Monte Carlo and high fidelity deterministic modeling techniques, Bob and his team were able to delivery a mechanical design that was robust to hardware-based variation. This is only one of hundreds of studies and projects that are providing robust and innovative design solutions to Xerox products.

Adding other Design for Lean Six Sigma Disciplines

In addition to the Electromechanical DfLSS program, we were anxious to start with two other groups critical to the overall success of efficient, effective and predicable product delivery: software and inbound marketing. Much of today's printer, copier and multifunctional device functionality is due to the sophisticated software associated with those devices. A significant portion of the total product development time and cost are tied up in the development and testing of that software. Given the important role in which software plays into the successful launch and outstanding performance of Xerox equipment, we felt it essential to develop a Software DfLSS program. Even with high performing, DfLSS trained design teams in place, there was still a discipline missing: inbound marketing. Without having extensive customer driven data on the customers' product expectations, we could be the best in the world at making products that no one wanted or needed. Therefore, soliciting and effectively capturing the voice of the customers and their respective expectations was essential for a successful product delivery. To facilitate these two new disciplines, we formed and chartered two DfLSS Core Teams and sent them off on their way to develop their respective curriculums. These two programs had their own unique challenges that will be the topic of future written works.

---

[i] Norman Fowler, *Moving Xerox + Lean Six Sigma to the next level with Design for Lean Six Sigma (DfLSS)*, WCBF Global Six Sigma Summit, Las Vegas, NV, June 28, 2006

[ii] Ken Embley, *The Burning Platform: Identification of the "burning issue" will encourage change in stakeholder behavior*, University of Utah, Center for Public Policy & Administration, Policy Perspective, Volume 1, Issue 1, March, 2005. http://www.imakenews.com/cppa/e_article000368179.cfm?

[iii] http://en.wikipedia.org/wiki/Delphi_method

[iv] Norman Fowler, Nabil Abu Gharbieh, George Maszle, Gilbreath Zealey, *"Lessons learned in the transition from Xerox Lean Six Sigma DMAIC to Design for Lean Six Sigma (DfLSS)"*, IQPC 7th Annual DFSS Conference, April 21, 2005.

[v] Norman Fowler, *Best Practices in Blended Learning: Xerox Design for Lean Six Sigma Development and Lessons Learned*, MoreSteam Users Conference 2006, South Bend, Indiana, September, 2006

[vi] Michael L. George, James Works, Kimberly Watson-Hemphill, *Fast Innovation*, New York, McGraw-Hill, 2005, pg. 63.

[vii] http://www.sigmazone.com/products.htm

[viii] http://www.airacad.com/LSSDesignFor.aspx

[ix] Andrea Shapiro, *Creating Contagious Commitment*, Hillsborough, NC, Strategy Perspective, 2003.

[x] Elaine Schmidt, *Duplicating Success: Xerox Reinventing Itself*, iSixSigma Magazine, Volume 2, Issue 5, 2006.

[xi] Bob Hildebrand, *Final Tollgate: Photoreceptor Belt Tensioning System*, iSixSigma Magazine, Volume 3, Issue, 2007.

Chapter 4 Lessons Learned: Hits and Misses

What worked, what didn't and what we found that was interesting

Working through the several years of Xerox DfLSS program development and deployment, there were several lessons that were learned. Some of the lessons were good, some were bad and others were interesting. Some outcomes were anticipated. Others were unintended outcomes (both positive and negative) of the decisions we made. I would caution people reading this that not all the lessons are directly transferable to all other companies and environments. These were outcomes of Xerox's work environment, excellent engineering competency and in a few instances what turned out to be just luck. These lessons learned could be considered like feedback; you can accept it, reject it or look into it. Some of these lessons may be transferable to your situation and most, if not all, should be looked into as companies begin to develop and deploy a Design for Lean Six Sigma program. Below are a series of those lessons with some explanation:

Start with Leadership

As with Xerox's successful DMAIC deployment, we lead DfLSS program deployment with training leadership first. It was essential to get Xerox management from the program design, development and delivery organizations to understand and buy-in to the overall DfLSS program. We knew going in that there was a fairly wide distribution of management opinions regarding Design for Lean Six Sigma ranging from strong DfLSS advocates to those who would not initially support the initiative. We utilized a two day management training session to expose management to process variation and how the DfLSS methods and tools could be used to minimize that variation, minimize rework as well as reduce product delivery times. We also exposed them to the suite of DfLSS software tools developed by SigmaZone, Incorporated described earlier. The training materials included trial versions of the software tools so managers could go back after the training and play with these new software tools. We spent time helping managers understand their important roles in the overall deployment and success of the program. This included an overview of the IDOV (Identify, Design,

Keys to Success

Training management first is critical because if you cannot get them on board, you will likely have problems implementing DfLSS within the rest of the population.

Optimize and Validate) process, key questions they would be expected to ask (and get answered) as well as the need for them to ask their employees to "show me the data!" This phrase was a key point that was reiterated constantly over the two training days. Without management asking for the data driven analysis there would not be the desired "pull" environment needed for this initiative to be successful. Fortunately, in many cases, "show me the data" stuck and had an immediate impact. As more managers asked for the data, researchers, engineers and other product delivery professionals started asking for, and in some cases demanding, training as soon as they could get it. This helped create the initial internal "buzz" necessary to help get the DfLSS program noticed and build the initial training demand.

Product Delivery Ownership.

The more that the DfLSS program is owned by the product delivery organizations, the better it is.

Xerox's DMAIC Lean Six Sigma program could be characterized as being led by a small, centralized Corporate Lean Six Sigma Office. This is not too different from many standard DMAIC Lean Six Sigma deployments. Though this proved effective for the Xerox's early years of deployment, we came to the conclusion that if Xerox was going to adopt DMAIC Lean Six Sigma as the "way we worked", there had to be a shift in ownership to the operational organizations and away from the centralized Lean Six Sigma Office. We still needed a formalized structure, framework and infrastructure in place (for such critical items such as

Keys to Success

By bringing design community representatives into the development process you make them part of the solution versus part of the problem.

certification, training, and other key functions) and managed centrally to ensure consistency and overall program success. However, the more the operations leaders internalized and actively participated in the overall governance of the program, the higher the probability for a pervasive and sustainable deployment.

This overall concept became even more important in our DfLSS deployment. As mentioned before, each product delivery organization, and even managers within those organizations, had different product delivery methods and techniques. Even though they all worked under the overall umbrella Xerox Time To Market process, within and across Divisions there still was a degree of process variability that made it difficult to converge on a single agreed upon set of program management methods and practices. This decentralized product delivery methods model also made it difficult for a centralized group, like the Corporate Lean Six Sigma Office, to have significant influence. This management independence made it difficult to push certain centralized function initiatives through the organization. We were faced with this scenario on numerous occasions and equated the frustration of driving important initiatives forward in this environment to "pushing on a rope." Though there were limited early successes, we were able to make more significant strides with the Division managers and their DfLSS Deployment Managers when they became more intimately involved in the overall DfLSS program governance. This can be a double edged sword, especially when there are widely divergent work processes, procedures and perceptions. But, as long as the participants are open minded and willing to listen to their design and development peers, things can be implemented smoothly.

Management "Rabbits"

Find those management "rabbits" and do what you can to make them successful.

We first saw this phenomenon during our DMAIC deployment, but it held true in our DfLSS deployment as well. What I mean here is find those managers who believe in the DfLSS principles and are anxious to get involved as early adopters. I am going to call these managers "the rabbits". Just like mechanical rabbits in a dog race, they lead the pack, run just out of reach and cause all the dogs to follow in hot pursuit. I do not mean any disrespect to the rabbits, dogs or managers, but the analogy seems to hold pretty true in Lean Six Sigma deployment. In Lean Six Sigma deployments, these rabbit managers help give the program credibility, they show all those who work for them that they are behind the Lean Six Sigma program and they help stir up some health competition between their peers. From my observations, the more senior the manager, the more competitive they seem to be. These managers typically like to win

Keys to Success

Tapping into management's competitive nature can be an asset in your overall deployment.

at work as well as with initiatives like Lean Six Sigma deployments. They like to be the first done with classes, score highest on the quiz, the first belt certified and be the first one recognized for their leadership. If you can tap into that competitive nature, it can help create a significant management pull for the overall program.

To support this competitive nature, the deployment community needs to do what they can to make these early adopting managers successful. This could include special coaching to help managers move through the material, visibility both upward and to their peers of their leadership and working with the managers to best select their personal projects and/or studies that fits their busy schedules. I am not saying one should make it easier or certification standards should be sacrificed to get these managers through classes or ultimately certified. That could actually have an overall negative impact on the program. I am however, supportive of giving these managers the help and support they need to set a positive example.

One impact we did not anticipate, but delivered a positive message was when we had a Division President sit through both weeks of Electromechanical DfLSS Green Belt training. To his credit, he sat through both weeks, actively participated in the exercises and took (and passed) the weekly quizzes like any other belt candidate. What made this special was it took away one of the most common excuses individuals in that Division for not participating: "I'm too busy." When managers and other people would say they were too busy to participate in the Design for Lean Six Sigma training, our response would be "are you busier than the Division President because he found time to complete the training." That was usually enough to them rethink how busy they really were.

The Training Trap

Do not get caught in the training trap

Though I bring this up within the context of Design for Lean Six Sigma, but it is equally applicable to any other Lean Six Sigma deployment. The training trap refers to having people believe that training is the end, not the means to a successful deployment. We caught our selves on multiple occasions during our Design for Lean Six Sigma development focusing a significant portion of our time and efforts on training and not enough on the other critical infrastructure and other factors necessary to our deployment. It is easy to be lulled into the feeling that developing the training is the "center of the deployment universe." Training is tangible, progress is easily measureable and it often tends to be a lightening rod for extensive and sometimes emotional debate.

Keys to Success

Though it is important, training is the means not the end of a successful Lean Six Sigma deployment.

An example of that lightening rod phenomena when we opened up the debate what type of Design of Experiment philosophy we would deploy in our program. Internal classical, fractional factorial and Taguchi subject matter experts joined in the extremely heated debate on which technique was best and should be taught in the Design for Lean Six Sigma training. These zealots were so focused on a debate which to include in the training that they lost sight of the fact a great deal of work was necessary to convince the general population to use *any* type of Design of Experiment. The more the non-value added Design of Experiments debate raged on, the more the subject matter experts lost sight of the real goal, of a successful deployment of the methods and tools across the product delivery population.

Even within the high level category of training, teams also can overlook important elements such as managing content change control, trainer certification and belt candidate registration and tracking because they focus too much on content structure and development. We found out the hard way that having the training, but not other essential elements in place when you launch can cause frustration for the early adopters and can damage the positive momentum that is critical in the early stages of a deployment. Therefore, one should not fall into the training trap and should spread their precious resources across all the components necessary for a pervasive and sustainable deployment.

Assess Current Capability

Take the time upfront to assess the current product delivery personnel competency and capability.

In parallel with the Electromechanical DfLSS program development, we took the time to assess various organizations' competency levels and the capability to absorb and utilize these new DfLSS methods and tools. We started by looking for those individuals or small pockets of excellence that were already using some or all of the DfLSS tools or methods. These people were critical to the program as they were called upon to validate the training content as well as enhancing the training with real life Xerox examples of how these tools and techniques have been used at Xerox to get impressive

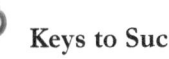

Keys to Success

Identify and leverage your DfLSS "pockets of excellence" as they are a critical asset. They can assist in curriculum development, provide company-specific tool usage examples and typically are advocates for your cause.

results. These pockets of excellence also served as DfLSS advocates who could interact with their peers, management and subordinates and help persuade those sitting on the fence that DfLSS was critical to product delivery success at Xerox. Having a Xerox employee stand up and share their successful study or project with their peers helped support the entire program by showing that these DfLSS tools and methods would work in the Xerox environment.

As much as we needed these pocket of excellence, they also needed the Design for Lean Six Sigma program to help validate to their management and peers that these engineers were approaching their work in an efficient and effective manner. We found that many of the people already utilizing the DfLSS principles and tools were doing so in a "stealth mode." They embraced Design of Experiments, Measurement System Analysis and other methods and tools, but typically did not draw attention to themselves. They knew the power of these methods, but also knew that not everyone (managers, peers and subordinates included) would embrace them as they did.

Keys to Success

In some cases, "pockets of excellence" advocates need DfLSS and its successful deployment as much as you need them.

It is amazing how much group norms and the desire to conform can have so much influence on individuals within an organization. Organizations were littered with people who had been designing products for decades in a less than optimum matter using methods such as one factor at a time experiments, no effective measurement systems in place, etc. These people had been recognized, rewarded and promoted for their approach. Despite these people and their less than desired approach, Xerox was able to deliver great products to the field, but usually at higher cost and design defects that had to be corrected after the product was launched. In the past as "one factor at a time" and "saved in the eleventh hour" product developers were rewarded, recognized and promoted it tended to push those who used DfLSS principles somewhat underground. Even though they knew the DfLSS principles were the more efficient and effective way to go, the pressures to conform to "the way it's always been done" were significant. So, these advocates would practice the tools individually or in small groups supporting one another and would not broadcast how they regularly were on time and on budget with a reliable working subsystem.

When the Design for Lean Six Sigma program came along, advocates for the DfLSS methods quickly recognized this as the platform they could use to validate how they approached their day to day work. All of a sudden, it was acceptable (and encouraged) to use the tools and disciplined approach that they secretly had been practicing for many years. These skilled people became "Product Delivery Rock Stars" practically overnight and for the first time, they felt accepted by the general product development community. As more people in their respective organizations got trained and practiced the DfLSS tools together, new group norms were forged embracing the same tools that once were shunned and forced underground. Before some "one factor at a time" developers realized, they were the minority and they felt the pressure to conform to the new way to work.

"CAVE" People

Watch out for the "CAVE" people.

In the Design for Lean Six Sigma management training, Air Academy Associates' President Mark Kiemele indicated that there are three basic populations when organizations deal with change: Pioneers, Settlers and CAVE people. Pioneers are often a small population where training alone is enough to empower them to adopt new initiatives. Settlers represent the largest and most significant population where training alone will not empower them. Settlers can also be characterized as "sitting on the fence" waiting to be convinced. The third population is known as CAVE people. The acronym CAVE stands for *"Citizens Against Virtually Everything."* These are the people who criticize anything new or different, even if it is a better way to do things. They want to keep things the way they always have been, do not want to rock the boat and typically do not accept a new ways of thinking. Fortunately CAVE people represent a small portion of the general population but they can have a significant negative impact.

Like any large corporation, Xerox had their share of CAVE people. At first, we listened to what they had to say. Often, some of the questions they asked and points they brought up were valid and needed to be addressed. One by one, we would sort through the comments and concerns and find ways to fix issues they brought up or put their comments aside. At some point however, companies need to "seal up the cave" and not let CAVE people out to "pollute" the Settlers pool. This can be done in a number of ways ranging from transferring them to other assignments to outright dismissal. The more Design for Lean Six Sigma becomes the way groups work and the accepted group norm, the more uncomfortable the CAVE people become. Eventually, CAVE people will either move on as they find the environment difficult to work in or they will huddle in their dark, damp caves alone.

Make Believers Successful

You are better off making "believers" successful than converting those who don't.

In today's business environment with the constant pressure to be more efficient and effective, it can seem we never have the level of resources we think are necessary to accomplish what we have been asked to do. For Xerox's Design for Lean Six Sigma Deployment, we were under a great deal of pressure to deliver our program with a constrained budget and deployment resources. This constrained environment created some anticipated deployment challenges but surprisingly also created a new set of opportunities that ultimately helped our overall deployment.

One such opportunity was focusing on the "believers." When we started our DfLSS deployment, our intention was to attempt to convert Xerox managers and other personnel to this new way of approaching their product development jobs. We quickly realized that that was a significant task and we did not have the resources to tackle everyone at once. We then shifted our emphasis to the believer population. The believer population included those who were already applying the DfLSS tools and methods, advocate managers and the previously mentioned Pioneers who will be empowered through just training. The focus was to take our precious resources to make these believers successful. This included giving training preferences to those managers who were strong advocates, supported the program and created an environment where trained DfLSS candidates could practice their newly acquired skills. We also made efforts to publicize those "believing managers" through a variety of internal media, showing the positive impact they and their reports made with DfLSS. For engineers, we documented testimonials and created videos that highlighted

Keys to Success

Helping those who believe in DfLSS to be successful can be a better use of your precious resources than trying to convince those who are not.

engineers and the outstanding work they were doing. This gave them exposure to their peers, immediate management and to upper management who became convinced that DfLSS was going to help overall product design productivity. This manager and engineer exposure enabled people who were "on the fence" to seek out DfLSS advocates and have face to face discussions. By making the believers successful, we made the entire DfLSS program successful.

For the ergs of energy expended, I believe we got an overall better payback by focusing on the believers than if we focused on convincing non-believers. As entire organizations, managers through engineers and technicians were trained and practicing their DfLSS skills, there became a bigger and perceivable performance gap between the believer organizations and those who did not. Smart "Settler" managers and engineers would see the gap, seek out their peers and get on board with the program. For those who choose not to embrace DfLSS, the performance gap grew to the point where certain actions to replace individuals were taken. In the end, we found it easier and more productive to make believers successful than trying to convert those who did not.

"DO" Loop

Do not let design engineers get caught in the "DO" loop.

Right from the beginning of our Design for Lean Six Sigma training deployment, there was resistance on several fronts to minimize the amount of time and effort placed on teaching the upfront portions of the IDOV process, especially items such as Voice of the Customer. Many product planners felt it was their responsibility to tell the design community what the customers wanted. Some even felt that they did not want researchers, designers and others involved in the product delivery community interacting with the customers at all. At the same time design engineers, excited about the set of Design for Lean Six Sigma software tools they just acquired and wanted to dive in and exercise their new Design of Experiment and Monte Carlo simulation capabilities. Some felt that they had always been told what to design and they did not want to be distracted by translating the Voice of the Customer or worrying about requirements flow down. In fact, many felt if they only worked on the Design and Optimize set of IDOV activities, they would be happy. We ended up calling this "caught in the DO loop."

We knew that we had to have the product design community fully versed in all elements of the IDOV process. First, without the true Voice of the Customer and the effective translation of product requirements, we could become the best in the world of making printers, multifunctional and other offerings that nobody wanted. All the Design of Experiments and simulations in the world could not make up for the fact that we missed what the customer really wanted in our products. Second, we wanted the design population well versed in the Identify phase activities, especially Voice of the Customer, so they knew the right questions to ask the product planning community when new or conflicting customer requirements were thrust upon them. Just as we taught the product delivery managers early on in our deployment, we wanted the design community to ask product planning to "show me the data." Our desire was to eliminate as much as possible people saying "I think this is what the customer wants" and replace it with "I know what the customer wants and here is the analyzed data to prove it." By having the design community pushing back on product planners for data and analysis such as prioritized customer requirements, conjoint experiment results and Quality Functional Deployment House one, it pressured the product planners to embrace their own Design for Lean Six Sigma curriculum for in-bound marketing. Just accepting a product planner's opinion was no longer going to be acceptable. The drive to get the design right the first time was predicated on the fact that the design

Keys to Success

Getting researchers, design engineers and others within the product delivery community closer to the customer and what they desire (or will come to desire) is a good thing.

community knew up front exactly what the customer wanted. That could only be done consistently over time by product planners and the design community embracing and jointly participating in the critical IDOV Identify activities.

At the back end of the IDOV process, some design engineers were not too excited about taking the time to validate their designs. Again, we pushed to ensure this phase was emphasized and kept in not only the curriculum but in managers' inspection of the design community's work. Even the most experienced Design of Experiment practioners find there are times where contributing factors are missed and analytical models do not necessarily agree with reality. Given a significant portion of Xerox's design community were still Design of Experiment novices, we needed to encourage them to validate their experimental designs to ensure critical inputs and factors did not slip through the cracks resulting in flawed models. This is especially true given the significant number environmental and process factors as well as interactions that influence and contribute to the xerographic process. Without validating their predicted subsystem, module or machine performance against actual, there is no way of ensuring that the models truly represent what will happen in the field. Once an offering enters the customer base, the cost associated with fixing a defect goes up exponentially so validating the design up front made good engineering as well as good business sense.

The validation step also served as a closed loop cycle of learning for those trying to master Design of Experiments. In my career, I must have had four or five different Design of Experiment courses. Although I learned a great deal about the mechanics associated with Design of Experiments sitting in the class room, I found I better internalized Design of Experiments when I rolled up my sleeves, got into the lab and set up, conducted and analyzed the experiments myself. I also found that I learned more when something went wrong and I made mistakes. Whether it is missing a critical factor, not randomizing my trails or any other ones typically made early on, mistakes allow us to challenge our assumptions and beliefs and build a stronger experience and knowledge base so we do not make them again in the future. Without the validation step, we cannot be sure our Design of Experiment models are correct and we miss out on a significant portion of the overall learning opportunity.

Therefore, resist the temptation of letting the design community focus solely on the IDOV "DO loop" and ensure they understand and fully participate in the important Identify and Validate process steps.

One Size Does Not Fit All

Recognize that one curriculum will likely not be applicable to all product delivery disciplines.

We learned the hard way that not all curriculums are necessarily applicable to all the different disciplines associated with successful product delivery. Like many other commercial and consumer products developed and delivered today, Xerox devices are made up of both electromechanical or hardware and software elements. In fact, more of today's product functions and overall capabilities are driven by software.

Xerox products are no exception. Though we knew there were fundamentally differences between the two initial DfLSS programs' content, the initial success of the Electromechanical program put a statistical tool bias on the Design for Lean Six Sigma Software content and curriculum. It took significant effort and time to convince the DfLSS Launch Team and leadership that the lower depth and breadth of statistics and the inclusion of Lean Software Development was appropriate for the Xerox software community. Some of this was due to the fact that we were treading on new ground with our Software DfLSS initiative and there were not many benchmark Design for Lean Six Sigma

Software programs developed or deployed. Some of the issues also had to do with the hesitation by a few Software DfLSS Core Team and software community members to accept *any* statistical tools. The DfLSS Launch Team felt strongly that for DfLSS to be successful and products to be delivered more effectively, efficiently and predictably, that all disciplines needed to have a

Keys to Success

There is a delicate balance between converging on common DfLSS program content and having enough flexibility to allow other product delivery disciplines (e.g. Software and In-bound Marketing) the content that better aligns to their specific job functions.

common "language." By that, when electromechanical engineers were talking about setting up a Design of Experiment and engaged the software and system engineers on critical set points controlled by software, everyone knew exactly what was being talked about. The debate on the depth and breadth of statistics in the Software Design for Lean Six Sigma curriculum became heated and emotional at times.

Finally, with the help of a Lean Six Sigma trained Master Black Belts who formally was a software developer we able to converge on a reasonable solution. She lead a DMEDI (DfLSS for process development) project aimed at capturing the Voice of the Customer and Voice of the Business and translating it to what level of statistics and overall content needed to be incorporated into the Software DfLSS program. This was a hard lesson to learn as time, momentum and a significant amount of resources were squandered delivering a curriculum and content that the software community was not going to embrace. A similar discussion and debate took place when we looked to develop a DfLSS curriculum for the in-bound marketing population. Looking back, we should have realized earlier that "one size will not fit all" and that there is a delicate balance that needed to be established between having that common DfLSS language, tools and methods and giving the appropriate content flexibility for each different discipline.

One thing that helped with that balance is having common terminology and tools. To help enable this all three disciplines (electromechanical, software and inbound marketing) were required to take MoreSteam.com's DMAIC Green Belt on-line training as a prerequisite to their instructor-led training. This helped establishing a common set of terms and the downloaded Excel®-based templates gave all disciplines a similar starting point. When it got to the DfLSS portion of the training, convergence on single set of terminology and practices became a bit more difficult.

When I sit back and look at the Lean Six Sigma community of consultants and training providers, it is sort of interesting that almost everyone has *converged* on the DMAIC and *diverged* on Design for Lean Six Sigma terminology and roadmaps. From all accounts, DMAIC has become an industry standard terminology and work process. However, if you look at Design for Lean Six Sigma providers you find a long list of different roadmaps. These include: IDOV (Identify, Design, Optimize and Validate), CDOV (Concept, Design, Optimize and Validate), DMEDI (Define, Measure, Explore, Design and Implement), DMADV (Define, Measure, Analyze, Design and Verify), DCDOV (Define, Concept, Design, Optimize and Validate), DVP&PV (Design Verification, Production and Process Validation) and the list goes on.

Each DfLSS provider has a different set of acronyms they use to separate their initiative from their competitors. However, if you put the roadmaps side by side, you find that most follow a similar set of basic steps and use similar methods. Even though there is some variability between roadmaps where phase boundaries are drawn, it appears that most DfLSS roadmaps are more similar than the different process acronyms would suggest.

We also found that most consulting firms specialized in one discipline or another and very few had electromechanical, software and in-bound marketing integrated together. This meant we had to bring in multiple consulting partners to deliver a fully integrated, multi-disciplined Design for Lean Six Sigma program. When we brought in different consulting partners in for the three different disciplines, we had to take the time and expense of converging not only the DfLSS roadmaps, but some of the tools they used so to our Xerox product delivery teams, they looked consistent. This meant changing consultant's training materials and exposing them to a different set of DfLSS software tools. This sounds easy, but it's not. It was a necessary step however to ensure consistency across the various disciplines.

Keys to Success

When you strip away all of the alphabet soup of DfLSS process acronyms, you find that there are more similarities than differences between the roadmaps.

Partner's Ability to Transfer Knowledge

Assess consulting partners on their ability to transfer knowledge within your own company culture and business situation.

As we went through the process of selecting our consulting partners, we developed a set of criteria that I imagine most other company deployment teams could have come up with. Criteria included elements such as workshop effectiveness, quality of the simulations and printed materials, capability to meet our training demand as well as overall cost. What we seemed to have underestimated when developing and using these criteria was *how* the consulting partner transferred knowledge with respect to the company's culture. One could argue that how consulting partners transfer knowledge is embedded and confounded in criteria such as workshop effectiveness. However, we found that it played a much bigger role on its own. When I say how knowledge is transferred, I am specifically referring to making sure that the training and coaching techniques, mechanisms and approach are consistent with a company's culture and how belt candidates are going to be motivated.

This became more obvious when consulting partner candidates, all very talented and who had successes at various other companies, presented their materials at Xerox. If you accept the assumption that the basic DfLSS tools and methods taught are very similar across various consulting partners, why would one firm be successful and the other not as effective? Why does one instructor do great at one company and the very next week fail at another? I found it hard to believe that all of a sudden the instructor forgot how to teach or lost all of their skills. After observing many different consulting partners and instructors within a particular consulting firm, I came to the conclusion that part of the answer lies in the consulting partner's ability to connect with a company's culture and what motivates its members. For some companies, discipline, order and logic would be enough to motivate students to adopt Design for Lean Six Sigma. For Xerox, that approach was not as successful with either our management or DfLSS belt candidates. My observations over five years of Lean Six Sigma training of Xerox product delivery personnel found that passion backed up by technical depth was what motivated our technical community. When I use the word passion, I am talking about being zealous and almost fanatical about Lean Six Sigma topics. I have seen "excitable" instructors as well as those who some would view as on the

Keys to Success

"How" a consulting partner transfers knowledge and connects with your company's culture is equally if not more important than "what" is transferred.

dull side, show that passion in different ways. What is funny about passion is that it can be infectious and spread through an entire class, sometimes without the class even knowing it. It is that instructor passion that spills over and makes belt candidates feel like they cannot wait to go to work and apply the tools they just learned. For some, it was that passion that helped many belt candidates resists the existing and somewhat dysfunctional group norms when they returned to their workgroups.

These next statements are not necessarily backed up by extensive statistical analysis and are based on my own observations. Therefore, they should be taken with a grain of salt. I have noticed that in many cases, that consulting firm employees tend to take on the characteristics of their firm's leaders. If the leader is passionate, there is a good possibility that their Master Black Belt trainers and coaches will also be passionate. If the leader is factual, logical and bland, it's highly likely that the employee Master Black Belts will be the same. This might be due to the halo effect (hiring a candidate because they have something in common with you) or for a number of other reasons. What ever the reason, I believe you can tell a great deal about the supporting Master Black Belts from the consulting firms' leaders.

Slow Down

Sometimes slowing down a deployment is a good thing.

As we began to deploy the Design for Lean Six Sigma curriculum, one of the challenges we had was to financially fit the program within the framework of our existing Lean Six Sigma budget. I was fortunate that my colleagues and manager saw the positive impact of the Design for Lean Six Sigma program and were supportive of the DMAIC funding and other tradeoffs we had to make. At the start, some Divisions took a "wait and see" attitude with respect to fully participating in the program. Once the first several DfLSS Green Belt waves were taught, coaching was in place and impressive results were seen, the number of people wanting to get into the program exceeded our ability to adequately fund the overall demand. As a result, we had to develop an allocation methodology for each Division and dole out the precious training seats. It was interesting to see, almost instantaneously, how much more valuable the training seats became when they were in shorter supply. We knew the negative impact of these financial constraints would increase the total time it would take to train the entire Xerox product delivery community. What was not necessarily anticipated were the positive impacts the constrained number of seats created.

> **Keys to Success**
>
> A wise Xerox Vice President once told me "if you give something to someone for nothing, it's worth nothing." Giving training seats real or perceived value can lead to positive design community behaviors.

When the DfLSS training constraint hit, the seats became a precious commodity. What could easily be gotten was now difficult to get. The more constrained the seats became; the more product delivery people wanted them. This created an increased "buzz" around the DfLSS program. Managers and other product delivery professionals started to push their DfLSS Deployment Managers for their allotted number of seats creating a competitive environment. This created an increased overall demand and even higher perceived value of each training seat. The increased demand drove the DfLSS Deployment Managers to stop and think very carefully when they assigned each training seat. Each training candidate and their working environment were carefully scrutinized. Will this training candidate have the supportive environment to ensure the training will stick? Will the training candidate's manager support this person and the entire DfLSS initiative? Will there be other trained candidates available to support this individual when they have completed training? Prior to the constrained number of seats, some Deployment Managers seem to randomly assign candidates based on who was available or who was convenient. When the constraints were imposed, each training candidate seat selection became much more strategic in nature.

In depth plans and strategies were put in place to maximize the value of each Division's individual training seat. One Division decided to focus on creating critical mass of trained personnel in subsystems that were historically less reliable or higher cost and had a manager who supported the DfLSS initiative. One other Division decided to train all the individuals working on one critical product. Each Division created their own detailed strategies on how to assign these critical training seats. As these strategies were executed, we saw a much more focused efforts on not only getting critical mass in certain organizations, but ensuring each trained candidate used their newly acquired skills and drove toward DfLSS Green or Black Belt certification. This helped to drive more completed studies which in turn resulted in more DfLSS success stories and certifications. As more senior managers began to ask appropriate DfLSS-based questions in various reviews, those who were Design for Lean Six Sigma trained were in a better position to correctly respond. The higher the number of success stories, the larger the gap between those groups who had been trained and those who were not. This resulted in more managers and their organizations wanting in to the DfLSS training thus creating even more DfLSS buzz within Xerox. As a result the training seats became even more precious and valuable. This helped build the DfLSS program momentum and keep it at a high level for an extended period of time. Without these funding and seat allocation constraints, I am convinced that many organizations would not have taken the training assignments as seriously as they did.

Having a Product Delivery Process Makes it Easier

As mentioned previously, Xerox had a well established product delivery process call Time To Market. Almost from the beginning, people began to ask if the DfLSS IDOV process (Identify, Design, Optimize and

Validate) was going to replace the Time To Market process. There was a great deal of discussion within the various DfLSS implementation and deployment teams how best to explain and illustrate the interdependency associated with both processes. After some pretty intense brainstorming, we were able to come up with a response that seemed to make sense. As a reminder, the Xerox Time To Market process was an end to end, phase gate product delivery process. As products move through the process, at each phase gate programs must demonstrate progress against various business, technical and other product-related readiness criteria. This results in a broad series of business and technology questions that needed to be answered and capabilities that needed to be demonstrated to successfully pass through each phase gate. At a high level, the DfLSS IDOV process defines how those technology-related Time To Market process questions will be met and readiness demonstrated. The DfLSS IDOV studies provide the fact based response to the technically-based Time To Market phase gate decision criteria. By separating the Time To Market "whats" from the Design for Lean Six Sigma "hows", we were better able to communicate how both processes coexisted in an efficient and effective product development environment. We also added the point that new product programs, senior program leaders and program design teams use the Time To Market process on a regular basis to assess the readiness of the entire product and major subsystems. However, a product delivery design engineer would be personally iterating the DfLSS IDOV process in their daily work to help support the Time To Market questions and requirements associated with the assemblies and/or parts they had responsibility for. It's not until one gets to the subsystem level that Time To Market and DfLSS IDOV actually would overlap. This is characterized in Figure 4.1.

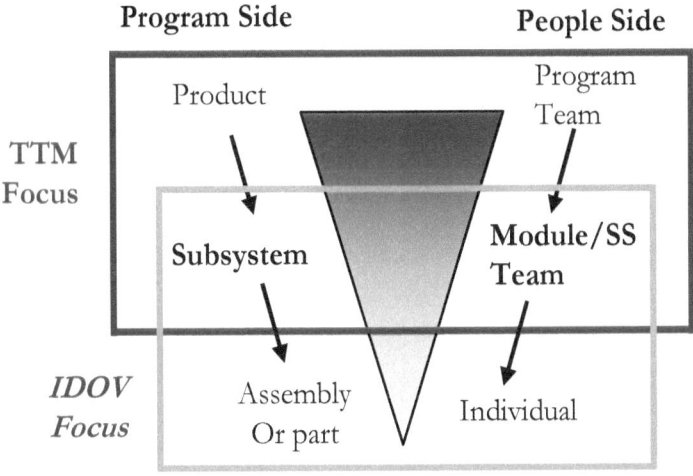

Figure 4.1: Xerox Time To Market and IDOV Integration

Having the Time To Market process in place actually helped the acceptance and ultimate integration of the DfLSS IDOV process. At the highest level, Time To Market's inherent discipline, phase gate approach was similar in nature to the Design for Lean Six Sigma process, so it was easy for the design engineers to understand, relate and respond to the new IDOV process. What was left for the DfLSS team to do was to create the links or hooks between the Time To Market "whats" to the DfLSS IDOV "hows." This was done by taking the technical-based Time To Market

Keys to Success

Without an established product delivery process in place the overall cultural acceptance hurdle became a bit higher as you have to incorporate DfLSS methods and tools in parallel with phase gate process discipline. That can be a lot for any organization to absorb all at once.

requirements and mapping in the set of DfLSS IDOV tools, methods and practices that responded to those requirements. The intent was to make it as easy as we could for development and design engineers to connect their individual Design for Lean Six Sigma studies to the overall product's Time To Market delivery process. What started as one of our most frequently asked and most difficult to answer questions, turned out to be one of our allies in connecting the past with the future DfLSS way of delivering products.

"In and Out" of Scope

Balancing what is "in" and "out" of the DfLSS scope can be difficult, so hold your ground.

We found it interesting how many people with their pet initiatives wanting to integrate them into the Design for Lean Six Sigma curriculum when it was perceived that the program was successful. We were continuously bombarded with people wanting to take what they believed was "essential" for the success of Xerox's product development and embed it into the DfLSS curriculum. It ranged from various development tools, sophisticated high fidelity modeling techniques and in some cases, topics that really did not even fit the DfLSS curriculum model. Though we listened to all the requests, we stood our ground and made only minor changes to the curriculum

Keys to Success

Saying "yes" to DfLSS content changes can be a very slippery slope. Look into each content change request and use "yes" wisely.

once we started. The issue was not that some of these suggested topics were not important. The rationalization to stand firm with the curriculum was based on several other factors. The fact that Air Academy had success with their curriculum with other clients in the past convinced us that they had solid content. We also were under a compress time constraint on overall training hours available. There was really no training session free or slack time and therefore adding even the smallest content would mean eliminating existing content to take its place.

With the exception of only these relatively small additions, we made very few changes from the Air Academy DfLSS content. The changes included a Xerox DfLSS burning platform in the beginning of training, roughly an hour of a reliability overview and some modeling reference materials placed in the appendix. We were under training time constraints because the Division Voice of the Business indicated that they could afford to keep product delivery personnel out Green Belt training for only two total weeks. We also knew that we wanted to expose the product delivery personnel to the power of the DMAIC process and Lean principles to supplement their on-line training. To enable that, we asked Air Academy to compress their normal 4.5 days of Fundamental training into four (Monday through Thursday). Luckily, the talent of Xerox's engineers enabled the faster overall pace. That left Friday for our one day DMAIC overview, introduction of Lean principles and having them run through three rounds of the simulation we use with our DMAIC Green Belts. That's a good deal of material for one week, but the students were able to manage it. We felt compressing the content any further to fit the two weeks would do more damage than good, so we stood firm on making changes.

Finally, saying "yes" to someone's pet project or content is a slippery slope because it makes it difficult to say "no" to the next person. It is interesting that just because you said "yes" to one person, independent of the quality of the idea, others feel they are entitled to the same "yes." I found this true during my DMAIC Green Belt deployment days when we were developing a new DMAIC Green Belt class for Executives. The changes we made to the basic DMAIC Green Belt content were based on the fact that managers had already been exposed to the simulation that is the cornerstone of the week long class during their leadership training. Our logic was that since they already knew the solution, it did not make sense to put them through the simulation again. By eliminating the simulation, it took almost a day out of the four and a half day training session. That meant that the Executive Green Belt would be roughly three and a half days. Our first Executive Green Belt class was going to be conducted in conjunction with an off site leadership meeting. The first request came from that management team to see if we could make the Green Belt training only three days as it better fit the schedule of events already planned. Working with our training partners, we developed a way it could be done so we said "yes." A few days later they asked if they could get another exception and make it two and a half, spread over three days so they could have their other meetings and their social events. The balance here was ensuring sufficient time to cover the basic materials as we were not interested in making the Executive Green Belt actually or perceived easier. The last exception request was to see if we could make the training two *long* days. Every time they came back to cut the time, it became more and more difficult to say "no." We finally settled on two plus days.

When get got the training feedback, students felt the overall class content and timing were acceptable, but the instructors felt too rushed and felt the negotiated structure would not work in the future. As we prepared for the next Executive Green Belt class, the next group found out about the first class's exceptions and asked if they could do it all in two days. Each new request was for less content and training time. Finally, we had to stay firm and say there would be no further exceptions made and the class would be three and a half days. It was a significant amount of non-value added discussions and work trying to accommodate a small group of belt candidates and the future Executive students felt slighted because they could not get the same deal as the first group. So, lesson learned, saying "yes" can be a very slippery slope.

Give Only What They Can Take
Only give people the amount of content and discipline that they can accept.

When we started to look at the entire body of DfLSS knowledge and what it would take to incorporate all the tools and a disciplined phase gate IDOV process, we realized that it was too much for the average design engineer or product delivery professional to internalize all at once. We also knew that if we tried to make immediate and significant changes in the overall product delivery work process, we would not be successful in the Xerox product delivery environment. With the authority given to the decentralized design function, there was little chance that a centralized staff organization was going to force any new tools or work process steps that product delivery management and engineers were not willing or ready to accept. So, we decided to start slow, limit the amount of material and overall process changes for certification and lead the design community over time to the overall answer.

That rationale was the basis for our DfLSS certification "study" strategy. Once belt candidates mastered the range of individual tools and methods, their curiosity and desire to learn more moved them to linking studies together into full blown DfLSS projects. Soon, Black Belt candidates were integrating individual transfer functions into system-level functions. People

Keys to Success

Giving organization's too much content and/or change all at once can result in none of it sticking long term.

banded together to integrate their individual studies into bigger and system-level projects. These practicing belts needed a management process in place, so they naturally adopted the IDOV phase gate process. Before we knew it, people were asking us for how they could implement these higher level tools, methods and process improvement steps. These were the same elements that we they would not accept if we pushed the activities on them from the start. This "stealth mode" deployment model was critical in our situation as it quietly pull in each of the product delivery and design-related organizations into the DfLSS process and helped give them more overall ownership in the program.

We knew Xerox had very dedicated and creative engineers, research and other assorted product delivery people who if given the chance would move toward the desired solution on their own. By giving the belts and their management smaller, "bite-sized" portions of the overall Design for Lean Six Sigma desired state and relying on their natural technical curiosity, we were able over time to help them move to the desired Design for Lean Six Sigma goal. Overall, the more they believed it was their idea to implement a particular tool, method or strategy, the better it was.

This overall Design for Lean Six Sigma migration concept can be graphically represented by Figure 4.2.[i] This diagram was first proposed by Jaime Soley, one of Xerox's Design for Lean Six Sigma Deployment Managers. It was then updated and modified with additional thoughts and higher complexity of DfLSS tools. As stated above, our intention was to start with studies built around fundamental DfLSS tools and

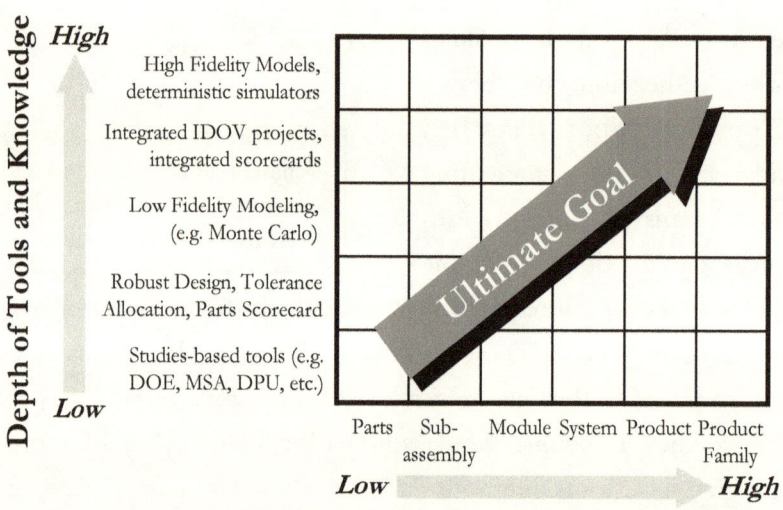

Figure 4.2: Depth of Tools and Knowledge versus System Level Pervasiveness

methods and a series of parts that each individual product design professional were working to develop. As the belt candidate mastered those tools, they typically looked to expand on their knowledge by adding more sophisticated tools (moving up the Y-axis) and applying that knowledge within an integrated set of parts or subassemblies (moving to the right on the X-axis). As individuals and groups of individuals moved toward the desired state (in the upper right corner) they mastered higher level concepts on higher level assemblies, ultimately leading to entire product-level integration.

The level of sophistication each person and/or group attained was based on their mastery of the next lower level and their desire to gain the next level of knowledge. We were convinced that pushing higher level tools and methods on individuals not prepared for those methods would have been a recipe for disaster, damaging the overall sustainability and pervasiveness of the DfLSS program.

Conclusion

My hope is that this book gives readers some insight into Xerox's unconventional Design for Lean Six Sigma development and deployment. For some, this may be a model for developing and delivering their own Design for Lean Six Sigma initiative. For others, this may give them a starting point for their own deployment or a few ideas on how they can enhance their existing deployment. At minimum, I hope readers can find a few "golden nuggets" that can be directly applied to in their own work environment to improve of their product delivery effectiveness, efficiency or predictability.

---

[i] Norman Fowler, *Moving Xerox + Lean Six Sigma to the next level with Design for Lean Six Sigma (DfLSS)*, WCBF Global Six Sigma Summit, Las Vegas, NV, June 28, 2006

Index